INSIGHT COMPACT GUIDE

GLASGOW

Compact Guide: Glasgow is the ideal quick-reference guide to Scotland's biggest city. It tells you everything you need to know about Glasgow's attractions, from its commercial and industrial heritage to its splendid museums and galleries, from its proud architectural landmarks to its peaceful parks and gardens, and from its sophisticated restaurant scene to the down-to-earth patter of the locals.

This is one of 130 Compact Guides, produced by the editors of Insight Guides, whose books have set the standard for visual travel guides since 1970. Packed with information, arranged in easy-to-follow routes, and lavishly illustrated with photographs, this book not only steers you round Glasgow but also gives you fascinating insights into local life.

Discovery

D1081265

Star Attractions

An instant reference to some of Glasgow's top attractions to help you set your priorities.

Cathedral p19

City Chambers p31

Princes Square p34

Tenement House p36

Kelvingrove Art Gallery and Museum p39

Pollok House p45

Glasgow School of Art p49

Loch Lomond p54

Burrell Collection p46

Burns Country p51

New Lanark p59

Introduction

Places

Culture

Leisure

Practical Information

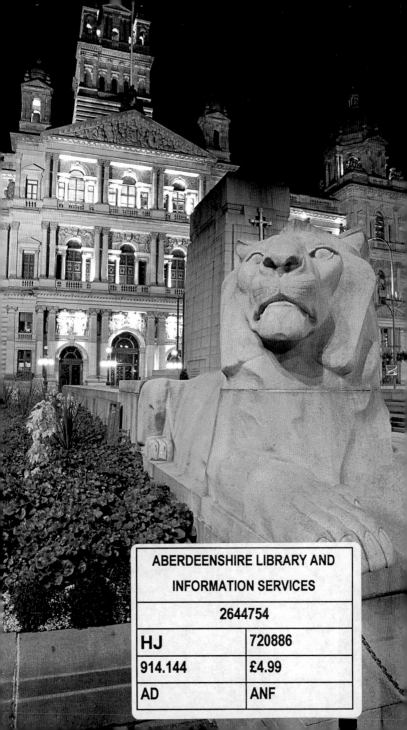

Glasgow – Scotland with Style

Glasgow is, in one sense, a Renaissance city. Like a strong and proud fighter who refuses to be knocked down, this vibrant, bustling, rumbustious Scottish city is once again busy reinventing itself.

Born as a fishing village on the slopes above the meandering River Clyde, Glasgow has been, in turn, a small market town, an ecclesiastical centre, a seat of learning, a city of merchant adventurers, a gateway to the New World, an industrial powerhouse of the British Empire and now a cultural capital of Europe.

But in all its guises – in its successes and in its troughs of depression – it has retained a robust and healthy sense of its place in the world.

Approaching from the south and looking down into the bowl of the Clyde valley, the first impression is discouraging. The tower blocks of the 1960s sprout like cubist mushrooms from the wide plain. On closer inspection, however, there emerges an architectural treasure house, with a mix of Victorian, Georgian, Venetian and art deco which equals anything in Europe.

Smart décor

5

Architectural grandeur

Through most of this century, the origin of the city's name – it is generally accepted to derive from the Gaelic *glas chu*, or Dear Green Place – was a source of wry amusement to the citizenry, who lived in grimy streets blackened by the soot of industry. When a former editor of *The Herald* first moved to Glasgow, he remarked, 'I arrived in a down-at-heel, demoralised town that seemed to perch on the edge of the civilised world with every chance of falling into the abyss.' In the middle years of the century, choking fogs enveloped the city, halting even the fondly remembered trams in their tracks.

The city retained its grim face until well into the second half of the 20th century, when the New Glasgow Society – a loose collection of early eco-warriors – led a rearguard action against the City Corporation's policy of 'If it's old, knock it down'. With the spur of their informed voices, the huge stock of Victorian tenement homes, apartment buildings constructed as cheap housing for immigrant workers in the East End and as more salubrious and spacious homes for the emerging middle classes in the West End, were stripped and refurbished instead of being demolished. This revealed a glory of honey-and-red sandstone with intricate masonry and striking detail. Even Glaswegians were surprised at how pleasant their Dear Green Place could be.

The defining moment in Glasgow's recent past was its selection in 1990 as European City of Culture after Athens, Paris and Berlin. The award came right on the heels of the enormously successful Garden Festival in 1988, and precipitated a year-long party of cultural events which sent civic confidence soaring.

After every party, unfortunately, there is a hangover, and in the 1990s the city drifted socially and economically. However, winning the title of UK City of Architecture and Design for 1999 provided fresh impetus for Glasgow to present itself as a cultural and artistic centre. Today the city is once again further reviving its fortunes with the bold regeneration of the inner-city riverbank, complete with smart riverside apartments, the new BBC building, the Clyde Arc bridge and, a seaplane service to Oban (tel: 0870 242 1457; www.lochlomondseaplanes.com).

An influx of important retail players, from Versace and Armani to Apple Computers and the huge Buchanan Galleries, also allows the city to compete as a major shopping destination, adding to the 500,000 visitors a year which it already attracts. Conference business has increased exponentially with the Scottish Exhibition and Conference Centre (SECC) on the north bank of the River Clyde and its adjacent aluminium-clad addition, (officially called the Clyde Auditorium) dubbed the Armadillo.

With the prospect of hosting the Commonwealth Games in 2014, Glaswegians are still getting used to the idea of visitors from abroad actually wanting to visit. Its reputation as a dour, violent slum persisted for so long that there is almost a measure of gratitude in the welcome for those who recognise it is rapidly shedding its dark past. A welcome there certainly is, not just from the city guides who keep an eye on tourists in the centre, but from the people on the streets who, consciously or not, like to live up to the civic slogan for Glasgow – Scotland with style.

Paolozzi sculpture at the Hunterian

6

Top name in design

Location

One of the backhanded compliments often paid to Glasgow is that it is so easy to get out of. The city lies in the wide strath, or plain, of the River Clyde and is sheltered to the north, east and south by high, open ground which provides an easily accessible rural playground. It is perfectly possible to be in rolling countryside within 20 minutes' drive from the city centre. It is about 26 miles (40km) from the sea at Greenock, and the Clyde starts to widen into the Firth just below the Erskine Bridge at Old Kilpatrick. The city is 45 miles (72km) by motorway from Edinburgh, the capital of Scotland.

Glasgow is situated on the same latitude as Labrador and Moscow, towards the west of the industrial central belt of Scotland. The Campsie Fells rise to 1,900ft (600m) to the north of the city and are dramatically visible from many areas.

Climate

The Gulf Stream warms the whole of the west coast of Scotland, and Glasgow is a beneficiary of more temperate weather than might be expected from its latitude. Winters are generally mild (between 0°C/32°F and 6°C/43°F) with more rain than snow, though cold snaps of up to -24°C (-11°F) have been experienced in the past decade. Summers, in common with the rest of Britain, appear to be growing warmer, with temperatures of up to 25°C (77°F).

The seaplane service to Oban

However, the prevailing westerly winds which blow across the Atlantic bring with them their fair share of rain, often in long and severe bursts, and the one constant in Glasgow weather is its unpredictability. A day which offers glorious sunshine in the morning can become a depression of drizzle by the early afternoon. Go prepared.

History of turmoil

Glasgow does not have a dramatic past. It is not a story of kings and courts and conflicts. In fact, it does not have much of a history to speak of until the 11th century, and it only contributed sparingly to the affairs of Scotland until the 17th century.

7

There is little doubt that the site was inhabited as long ago as 4000BC, when hunters pushed north in the wake of the retreating ice. It almost certainly owes its existence to the presence of shallows in the Clyde, by which the river could be manageably crossed.

The Roman general Agricola found hostile tribes in the area when he advanced from Britannia in AD80 and threw up a chain of forts across the narrow waist of Scotland. This line of defence was redrawn in about AD142 when the Antonine Wall was built across the north of present-day Glasgow.

The retreat of the Romans led to centuries of turmoil between flowing, warring tribes of Scots, Picts, Britons and Angles, and some more romantically inclined historians say the Glaswegian man's characteristics of quick aggression and pride in toughness can be traced back to the struggle for existence against incessant marauding.

Glasgow Cathedral

St Ninian began missionary work in Strathclyde in the 4th century, but St Mungo is credited as the founder of the city in AD543, although only legend bears witness to his arrival. A fine legend it is, too, with the holy man – who was led to *glas chu* by two white bulls and proclaimed bishop – performing miracles at the drop of a mitre.

Glasgow Cathedral was founded in 1136 on the site of St Mungo's Church on the banks of the Molendinar, a pretty *burn* (stream) which the Victorians later covered over and used as a sewer. Glasgow University was created in 1451. But, although the city was recognised as a respectable seat of learning with strong religious traditions

Civic dignitary in the Trades Hall

Tobacco merchant's mansion in Greenbank Garden

throughout the Middle Ages, all the political and military action took place in Edinburgh, which lay in the path of invading English armies, and in Falkirk and Stirling, where Scots nobles fought out their endless squabbles.

For many years the city owed much of its *raison d'être* to the Cathedral and the sway of the bishop. But the establishment of the colonies across the Atlantic, which opened up new markets, triggered its transition to the industrial, secular town of later centuries. The great barrier was its distance from the sea, and as far back as the 1560s desperate attempts were being made to cut through the sandbanks of the river. It was not until two centuries later that John Golborne's ingenious plan – to build piers along the banks and allow the river to scour its own bed – turned Glasgow into a serious contender as an Atlantic port.

Industrial awakening

The first great merchants were the Tobacco Lords, many of whose houses still stand. They created not only the tobacco trade with Maryland, Virginia and North Carolina, but a merchant class whose vision was matched by its arrogance and power. Their need for iron tools, glass, pottery and clothes to trade back to the colonies was the impetus for the city's awakening to the Industrial Revolution.

Glasgow became a cotton town in 1780, when weaver James Monteith discovered the secret of cheap imitation muslin. Within a decade, scores of mills were using the fast Scottish rivers to power their looms, and immigrants from Ireland and the Highlands were flooding in to share in the work. But the machinery was still largely imported from Europe, and the need to partake in the new knowledge spawned a breed of early technocrats whose impact was felt far beyond their shores – James Watt (1736–1819), inventor of the condensing engine; William Murdock (1754–1839), inventor of gaslight; William Kelly, inventor of the water-powered spinning jenny in 1792; and J.B. Neilson (1792–1865), inventor of the hot blast process for iron.

As it embraced the revolution, Glasgow's population exploded, from 23,500 in 1755 to a peak of 1,128,000 in 1939. The metal-bashing industries – shipbuilding, ironworks, armaments – were complemented by textiles, chemicals and manufacturing, and the city disappeared under the pall of enterprise. The English novelist William Makepeace Thackeray remarked in 1852, 'What a hideous, smoking Babel it is.'

The Victorians brought great enterprise, great hardships and great benefit: always with one eye on profit, the entrepreneurs also had time to consider the public well-being. One of their legacies to the city is a water supply from Loch Katrine which is good enough to be bottled and sold.

'Let Glasgow Flourish' – mosaic in the City Chambers

During the 20th century, Glasgow shared in the spoils and misfortunes of the industrialised world. The decline of heavy industry hit hard, but, as in generations past, the city has searched for opportunity in misfortune. There may be no more belching foundries, and the clang of the hammer is all but silenced in the shipyards, but recent city administrations have pragmatically courted private finance and quietly found new, previously unexplored areas of enterprise. Smart new hotels and luxury riverside apartments are springing up, bringing with them a new sense of civic pride. Tourists now go unremarked in the summer streets; retail, services and design provide jobs for a jaunty, smartly dressed and prosperous people. Glasgow is flourishing once again.

Finnieston Crane on the Clyde

The people

Glaswegians have a way with words, even if visitors have difficulty understanding them. Fast, snappy retorts are a greater delight to them than the sharp aggression with which reputation burdens them.

One man and his dog

The patter, sociologists would argue, is a mix of native sharpness, Highland feyness, Jewish morbidity and the Irish *craic* (witty story-telling). Much of Glasgow's story has been harsh, and, in the past, raising a laugh served as an antidote to adversity. The shipyards of the 1960s provided plenty of material for Glaswegian-born comedian, Billy Connolly.

But the people of Glasgow have an almost instinctive inquisitiveness about strangers and an inborn tendency to take people at face value which has not changed over the centuries. The Victorian novelist Charles Dickens remarked after a visit to the Athenaeum in 1847, 'I have never been more heartily received anywhere or enjoyed myself more completely.' It is hoped that this sentiment is perpetuated.

A Glasgow welcome

9

Historical Highlights

From 4000 BC Early settlements form at fords across the Clyde to take advantage of salmon-fishing and rich game pickings of Strathclyde. In the Bronze Age, settlers leave burial mounds near Pollok House and Cathkin Braes.

AD 80 Roman general Agricola builds a camp at Barr's Hill near Kilsyth as a defensive measure against the Picts.

142 Antonine Wall is built in the reign of Emperor Antoninus Pius through Duntocher, Bearsden and Kirkintilloch to the north of the city.

400 St Ninian consecrates a Christian cemetery near the banks of the Molendinar Burn which flows into the Clyde.

543 St Kentigern – also known as St Mungo – founds a church on the site of St Ninian's cell which becomes the leading Scottish centre of Christian culture, aided by contacts with Ireland.

1124 Between 1124 and 1136, the first cathedral is built on the site of St Mungo's Church.

1164 Bishop Herbert defeats Somerled and the armies of the isles in a decisive battle at Renfrew.

1175 The town is constituted as a burgh and the jurisdiction of the bishop established.

1189 The first cathedral is destroyed by fire.

1190 The Glasgow Fair, which is still celebrated as a holiday, is established.

1199 Glasgow successfully resists claim of jurisdiction from the Archbishop of York and secures from the Pope the decision that the Scottish and English Churches were separate and distinct.

1226 Charters are issued to prevent other burghs taxing Glasgow's trade.

1270 Consecration as bishop of Robert Wishart, who became a central figure in the war of independence against Edward I of England.

1297 Scottish hero William Wallace fights the English at the Bell o' the Brae in the High Street.

1350 First bridge is built across the Clyde by Bishop Rae. It lasted with various alterations for nearly 450 years.

1451 Establishment of the University of Glasgow, in College Lands east of the High Street under a papal bull secured from Pope Nicholas V through the offices of Bishop William Turnbull.

1491 Pope Innocent VIII makes Glasgow an archbishopric equal in status to St Andrews.

1560 Church of Scotland is established by law.

1566 First attempt to gain access to the sea when labourers from Dumbarton, Renfrew and Glasgow try to cut a channel through the Clyde sandbanks at Dumbuck.

1568 Glasgow backs Regent Moray at the Battle of Langside.

1578 Reformation persuades magistrates to demolish the cathedral. Craftsmen rally to the defence of the building.

1611 Glasgow becomes a royal burgh.

1626 New Tolbooth building is started. All that now remains is the steeple.

1696 Glasgow suffers heavily in ships, money and human life with the failure of the Darien Scheme, an ill-fated attempt to establish a Central American bridgehead to the colonies.

1707 Union of the Scottish and English parliaments, which is vigorously opposed in Glasgow and leads to violent riots.

1745 Bonnie Prince Charlie's army descends on the city and holds it to ransom for 10 days.

1752 The Hodge-Podge Club – frequented by soldier Sir John Moore, editor Samuel Hunter and trader Kirkman Finlay – is founded in the golden age of Glasgow clubs.

1755 The Saracen's Head – the oldest hotel in Glasgow – opens for business, established by Robert Tennent, founder of the brewing family.

1763 Development of coal and iron fields in Lanarkshire promotes rapid growth and lays the foundation of Glasgow's industrial importance.

1773 John Golborne of Chester opens Glasgow to the sea by building a series of jetties along the Clyde, allowing it to scour a channel in its own bed.

1783 The *Glasgow Herald*, now *The Herald* and the oldest English-language national daily newspaper, begins life as the *Glasgow Advertiser*.

1790 Opening of the Forth and Clyde Canal.

1793 The Session House and Tron Church are destroyed by flames after members of the Hellfire Club compete to see who could stand closest to a fire that was out of control.

1806 Death of David Dale, who with his son-in-law Robert Owen, created New Lanark cotton mills, practising enlightened care of their workers.

1809 Glasgow-born general Sir John Moore, famed for his humane treatment of his troops, is killed at Corunna.

1828 J.B. Neilson introduces hot blast furnaces, a fuel-economic method which becomes a cornerstone of the Industrial Revolution.

1833 Glasgow Necropolis, modelled on the Père Lachaise cemetery in Paris, is opened.

1859 A new water supply from Loch Katrine supplies clean drinking water to the city.

1865 The last public hanging, in front of a crowd of 30,000. Joseph Lister successfully uses carbolic acid antiseptic for the first time during surgery at the Royal Infirmary.

1866 The transformation of the city from an ecclesiastical centre into a commercial one is exemplified by the abbreviation of the civic motto 'Let Glasgow Flourish by the Preaching of Thy Word' to 'Let Glasgow Flourish'.

1867 The founding of the new university on Gilmorehill, incorporating some relics of the old High Street College.

1870 Tramcars are introduced. The last one ran in Glasgow in 1962.

1877 The Mitchell Library is opened in Ingram Street. It moved to North Street in 1911 and is the largest public reference library in Europe. An explosion kills 230 miners at a pit in High Blantyre.

1883 The Boys' Brigade is founded in a Free Church Mission Hall by William Smith.

1888 The International Exhibition held in Glasgow is followed by the erection of the Art Gallery in Kelvingrove Park.

1898 The People's Palace, inspired by the ideas of William Morris and John Ruskin, opens as a cultural centre for working people.

1926 Glasgow hit by the General Strike.

1941 Horrific toll of casualties as German bombers blitz Clydebank and Glasgow.

1958 Sir William Burrell dies at 87. His shrewd and idiosyncratic collection passes to the city and is housed in an impressive new building in Pollok Park in 1983.

1962 St Andrew's Halls, Glasgow's first concert halls, are destroyed by fire. The facade has been preserved at the Mitchell Theatre.

1967 The last of the great liners, *Queen Elizabeth II*, is launched at Clydebank. Celtic become the first British team to win the European Cup after beating Inter Milan 2-1.

1971 66 football fans are killed and 145 injured in a stampede at Ibrox stadium.

1982 Pope John Paul II visits Glasgow to a welcome by 250,000 people in Bellahouston Park.

1990 Glasgow chosen as European City of Culture. The resulting influx of visitors helps set the city on a new course as a tourist destination.

1999 Glasgow becomes UK City of Architecture and Design.

2001 Glasgow Science Centre opens.

2007 Kelvingrove Museum and Art Gallery reopens after a multi-million pound refurbishment. Glasgow–Oban seaplane service commences.

Botanic Gardens

M8

Dobb

Park Circus

Woodlands Road

New City Road

West Graham Street

Kelvingrove Park

Tenement House

45

Garnet St

Scott St

Buccleuch

Street

Hill St

Dalhouse Street

Rose Street

Street

Street

Cowcadden

U Cowcaddens

Woodside Place

5

Renfrew

Glasgow School of Art

M

Sauchiehall Street

Cambridge

Street

Street

Kelvingrove Art Gallery and Museum

North Street

Berkeley Street

The King's Theatre

43

Bath Street

Blythswood Street

W. Campbell Street

M
The Willow Tea Rooms

Renfield Street

Ba

Mitchell Library

44

Kent Road

Elmbank St

Holland St

Pitt Street

Douglas Street

Wellington Street

St Geo

5
St Vincent Street

Hope Street

41

St Vincent St Free Church of Scotland

Glasgow Stock Exchan

42

Hilton International

Bothwell Street

Waterloo Street

The Roga

Princes S

Union St

St West

Clydeside Expressway

Central Station

The Lighthouse M

Mitchell

M8

Argyle

Street

U
St Enoch

Anderston Quay

J Watt St

York Street

Oswald Street

Jamaica Street

St E
Shop
Cer

Scottish Exhibition and Conference Centre

Kingston Bridge

Broomielaw

George V Bridge

Bridge St

Glasgow Bridge

R i v e

Paisley   Road

Kingston

Commerce St

Street

Nelson Street

Sherif
Court

Glasgow Science Centre

Wallace Street

Norfolk Street

U
Bridge St

West Street

Cook Street

Eglinton Street

Bedford Street

Citizen's
Theatre

Scotland Street

West St
U

Gorbals

C

M8

Kilbirnie Street

ROUTES 1 – 5

0   250 metres

0   250 yards

N

15

Glasgow Caledonian University

Kennedy Street

Baird Street

Loan

Calgary Street

Kyle Street

Road

Springburn Road

Alexandra Parade

St Mungo Avenue

Stirling Road

Castle Street

Killermount St

39 Glasgow Royal Concert Hall

38 Buchanan Galleries

North Hanover Street

Cathedral Street

Strathclyde University

Provand's Lordship

9 Royal Infirmary

Glasgow Cathedral

10

Necropolis 11

Campus Village

7

8 St Mungo Museum of Religious Life and Art

U Buchanan St

Queen St Station

4 Merchants' House

40

George Sq.

32

28

30 Glasgow Tourist Office

31

Gallery of Modern Art

George Street

City Chambers

29

Italian Centre

26 25 Hutchesons' Hall

Trades Hall 27

Glasgow Sheriff Court

Cochrane St

Ingram Street

24

22 Ramshorn Kirk

23 21 Old Fruitmarket

City Halls

High Street Station

4

3

Barony Hall

5 Cathedral Sq.

6 Glasgow Evangelical Church

Duke Street

High Street

Rottenrow

Wishart Street

Barrack Street

Glassford St

Candleriggs

Albion Street

Wilson St

Bell St

1

Tolbooth Steeple

2

3

1 Mercat Cross

Trongate

Tron Theatre

20

Osborne Street

Stockwell Street

Saltmarket

Bridgegate

St Andrew's Parish Church

16

2

The Barras

12 The Saracen's Head

13

Gallowgate

Ross St

Kent St

Bain St

London Road

Greendyke Street

High Court

Victoria Bridge

17 Central Mosque

2

Albert Bridge

Crown Street

Glasgow College of Nautical Studies

Ballater Street

Lauriston Road

Street

15 Doulton Fountain

14 People's Palace

Glasgow Green

Templeton's Business Centre

C l y d e

M The Mackintosh Tour

Above: Glasgow Cathedral
Preceding pages: Clyde
Auditorium

Route 1

The High Street

High Street – Castle Street – Cathedral Square – Provand's Lordship – St Mungo Museum of Religious Life and Art – Necropolis *See map, pages 14–15*

The Mercat Cross was the centre of social and economic life in Glasgow for many centuries. It was the domain of traders and merchants who looked after matters temporal while the clergy of the Cathedral, further up the hill on the banks of the Molendinar Burn, concerned themselves with matters spiritual. The Mercat Cross was the visible evidence of a burgh's right to hold a market.

Mercat Cross

There is no clear evidence of where the original ★★ **Mercat Cross ❶** stood, and the squat octagonal building with a unicorn-topped pillar which now stands on the intersection at Glasgow Cross is a replacement erected in 1929. The Mercat Building behind it is, despite its Chicagoesque appearance, a warehouse built in 1925.

Starting our walk here, the cross is dominated by the ★★ **Tolbooth Steeple ❷**, which lies stranded in the middle of busy traffic where the High Street passes into Saltmarket. The Tolbooth was once an integral part of civic life in Glasgow and has occupied this site in various forms since the earliest days. Its functions were manifold, from a meeting place for the town council, to a tax collection point, courthouse and jail.

Tolbooth Steeple

The square tower was part of a five-storey building which extended west along the Trongate, towards the steeple of **Tron-St Mary's** *(see page 26)*, and its buttressed crown houses the latest of a fine carillon of bells which, in the 18th century, played out a different Scottish melody every two hours. The present bells, installed in 1881, were tended by hereditary bell-ringers, the last of whom, Jessie Herbert, rang the bells until 1970. Their annual high point was, of course, marking the Hogmanay celebrations which saw vast crowds welcoming the New Year in boisterous fashion. The Hogmanay party now takes place in George Square, to the sound of rock bands.

If spirits haunt any part of Glasgow, it should be here. Men – and women – were hanged outside the Tolbooth, and witches and miscreants scourged. The original building had spikes on the walls for the decapitated heads of felons. When the justiciary decamped to its new home at the river end of the Saltmarket and the council moved west, the main part of the Tolbooth was lost, and only the steeple and its winding stone staircase remain.

The High Street runs north past Victorian tenements (1883), with shops below on the left and new flats converted from old warehouses on the right. The street names offer clues to the past: Blackfriars Street, from the 13th-century Dominican monastery (there is a popular pub and hotel here on the right called Babbity Bowster, tel: 0141 552 5055); Bell Street, after Provost Sir John Bell (1680); and College Street, denoting the **Old College** which was sited here until the middle of the 19th century.

17

A popular watering hole, the name Babbity Bowster derives from an 18th-century dance

The University of Glasgow was established by Bishop William Turnbull in 1451 and flourished for the next few centuries in a pleasant environment between the High Street and the Molendinar Burn. It was here that Adam Smith, author of the seminal work on laissez-faire economics, *The Wealth of Nations*, was appointed Professor of Moral Philosophy in 1752. The university moved west in 1870 *(see pages 41–42)*, and the site was sold to the City of Glasgow Union Railway Company, which demolished it and erected the College Goods Station, which has now also gone, leaving this area to undergo imminent redevelopment.

On the left, opposite the High Street Station, is the shell of the old **British Linen Bank**, which has a statue of Pallas, goddess of wisdom and weaving, and a plaque on the corner recalling that the poet Thomas Campbell frequented a coffee shop on the site. Close by, on Nicholas Street is the College Bar, Glasgow's oldest pub (est. 1515).

Crossing George Street and curving up the hill, the street is flanked by excellently restored tenements with crow-stepped gables, turrets and balconies. On this hill, the Scots freedom fighter William Wallace – glorified by Hollywood and Mel Gibson in the film *Braveheart* – fought a running battle with the English forces in 1297.

★ **Barony Hall ❸** in **Rottenrow** (Saturday and Sunday) is the first major building of the Cathedral complex

The sandstone Barony Hall

and opens out onto Castle Street. It was built in 1889 from beautiful red sandstone and graced with slender stained-glass windows and a grey Gothic spire. It is now owned by the University of Strathclyde, and on graduation days the street teems with begowned students and tutors making their way to the hall to receive and bestow degrees.

Rottenrow is one of Glasgow's earliest streets, and its name has never been adequately defined, with suggestions as far apart as *route de roi* (king's way) to *vicus ratonum* (street of rats). It leads to the university's ★ **Campus Village ❹**, a pleasing and colourful student quarter built over the past two decades, proving that not all modern architecture is unsympathetic.

The Campus Village

Opposite the Barony Hall is ★ **Cathedral Square ❺**, guarded by an equestrian and rather imperious statue of William of Orange which was resited by the Provincial Grand Black Chapter of Scotland in 1989 from the Trongate, where it suffered terrible indignities each Hogmanay. It is said that the tail of King Billy's horse was broken off by a reveller and replaced with a ball and socket joint, with the result that on particularly stormy days, the tail can be seen to wave in the breeze.

On the south side of the square is the 1960s Ladywell housing estate, built over the medieval well of that name and the former Duke Street jail. The east side is bounded by the ★ **Glasgow Evangelical Church ❻**, which features life-sized statues of the Apostles. Just to the north, more worldly pleasures can be found at the **Cathedral House**, a small hotel housed in a red sandstone building, dating from 1896, which has an interesting three-level bar.

Provand's Lordship

The oldest dwelling-house still standing in Glasgow is ★★ **Provand's Lordship ❼** (Monday to Saturday 10am–5pm, Friday to Sunday 11am–5pm). It lies opposite Cathedral Square and was built in 1471 by Bishop Andrew Muirhead to house the master of the hospice of St Nicholas, who looked after a complement of 12 old men.

The house was saved and restored in 1906, with financial aid and period furnishings supplied by Sir William Burrell *(see page 46)* in 1927 and is now run by Glasgow Museums. Behind it lies a **Physic Garden**, in tribute to St Nicholas. The sound of the traffic gives way to medieval calm here, among the herb plantings and knot gardens. Behind the wall, towards the Strathclyde campus, is a small but ambitious orchard, where students convene under the spring blossom and try to ignore the M8 just up the road.

St Mungo Museum: plaque

Back across the High Street – traffic is always particularly bad here – is the ★★ **St Mungo Museum of Religious Life and Art ❽** (Monday to Saturday 10am–5pm, Sunday 11am–5pm, admission free), which caused some controversy before it was opened in 1993 over whether it was an architectural pastiche. The honey stone building houses works of art from the main religions – Buddhist, Christian, Hindu, Jewish, Muslim and Sikh – as well as many minor ones. The museum's pleasant coffee shop backs onto an attractive Zen garden designed by Yasutaro Tanaka which is another unexpected haven of peace in this busy street.

The cathedral precinct is fronted by a statue of Scots missionary explorer David Livingstone *(see page 57)* and provides an excellent foreground for the massive bulk of the ★ **Royal Infirmary** , which was completed in 1915 and commemorates the 65-year reign of Queen Victoria, whose solemn presence looms above the entrance. The Royal, which has been operating since 1794, has made a proud contribution to world medicine: Lord Lister pioneered antiseptic surgery here in the 1860s; Sir William Macewen established his reputation in brain surgery and osteopathy here in the 1890s; and his matron Mrs Rebecca Strong introduced the world's first systematic training for nurses. In the early part of the 19th century, its resources were stretched to cope with epidemics of cholera, typhus and dysentery. It also has one of the busiest casualty departments in Europe, coping with Glasgow's still prevalent weekend bouts of random and inventive violence. One casualty surgeon remarked that it was one of the few cities in Europe where patients still came in with sword wounds.

The Royal Infirmary

19

At the east end of the precinct lies ★★★ **Glasgow Cathedral** (April to September, Monday to Saturday 9.30am– 5pm, Sunday 1–5pm; October to March, Monday to Saturday 9.30am–4pm, Sunday 1–4pm). The tides of history have washed over this important ecclesiastical site since Glasgow's early days. It was founded in 1136

Glasgow Cathedral inside and out

Stained glass in the Cathedral

The Necropolis

John Knox remembered

> Tity. Disinterestedness, and Courage
> ood unshaken in the midst of Trials
> Maintenance of the highest Objects
> Finally.
> reasing Reverence for the Principle
> s of that Great Reformation, hrc
> ce of which our Country, hrc
> Midst of Difficulties.
> nour, Prosperity, and Happin
> s Erected by Voluntary Contr
> Memory of JOHN KNOX;
> sent under God, of the Ref
> on the 22ⁿᵈ day of Septem
> in the faith of the Gospel
> ber A.D. 1572, in the 67ᵗʰ

on the site of St Mungo's Church and has always been a focus for Christian learning and culture in Scotland.

It has stood through the supremacy of the bishops, the War of Independence and the upheaval of the Reformation, and began to take the shape which we see today around the middle of the 14th century. The main structure is a rectangle with a cross surmounted by a tower and steeple. A lower church opens up underneath the choir.

Its blackened stone illustrates the colouring of many Glasgow buildings before stone-cleaning became widespread. Attempts have been made to clean it up, but it was felt that it would cause too much damage.

The visitors' entrance is flanked by a memorial to the Hutcheson brothers *(see page 30)* and George Baillie, who 'divested himself of his fortune to endow institutions devoted to the intellectual culture of the operative classes'. The grounds are surrounded by gravestones.

At the south side of the Cathedral is a bridge which spans Wishart Street and leads to the ★ **Necropolis** ⑪, an impressive ornamental garden cemetery modelled on Père Lachaise in Paris. It is full of crumbling temples and monuments. The bridge was built by the Merchants House of Glasgow to 'afford a proper entrance to the new cemetery combining convenient access to the grounds' and views of 'the venerable Cathedral and surrounding scenery'. Indeed, the views of the Cathedral from the hill formerly known as Fir Park not only give some idea of the imposing grandeur of the Cathedral in medieval times, but also afford superb vistas as far as Ben Lomond to the north-west and the Cathkin Braes to the south. Roe deer can be seen roaming in the Necropolis.

Paths lead in circles round the hill past gloomy, ivy-clad, marble-pillared tombs and sombre obelisks. The Victorians took themselves as seriously in death as in life. The crowning monument on the summit is to John Knox, the austere father of the Reformation which 'produced a revolution in the sentiments of mankind', who still keeps a suspicious eye on the city below.

Leaving the cemetery in Wishart Street, the route passes the huge steel tanks of the Tennent Caledonian Brewery, which supplies a commodity as welcome to Glaswegians as Loch Katrine's water. At the foot of the street the modern flats and high-rise blocks on the right stand on the site of the Drygate, one of the original streets of old Glasgow.

Turning right into Duke Street, past the former Alexander's School, now a business centre, which features heads of Shakespeare and other luminaries on its frontage, the route follows along the wall of the old College Goods Yard. To return to Glasgow Cross, turn left at the traffic lights into the High Street.

Route 2

Fountain detail on Glasgow Green

The Barras and a short stroll south of the Clyde

The Barras – The People's Palace – Glasgow Green – River Clyde – Central Mosque – Saltmarket *See map, pages 14–15*

Saturday or Sunday is the best time to undertake this route, as the majority of shops around the Saltmarket are open.

If the High Street is redolent of Glasgow's past, The Barras is all about the way people live today. Although at first glance this busy marketplace is tatty and run-down, the area is full of life and colour, and bargain-hunters flock to it from all over the city and beyond. This route can be walked comfortably without stops in 45 minutes.

Starting the walk from the **Mercat Cross** *(see page 16),* head east up the **Gallowgate**, which is generally accepted to have the macabre meaning its name implies. However, the late historian George Eyre-Todd suggested that it meant the *gait,* or way to, the *gia lia,* or sacred stone of Celtic times, which would make it one of the oldest roads in Scotland. Social raconteur Jack House recalls days in the 1930s when the street housed 60 pubs and he 'never ventured there without an occasional *frisson* disturbing me'.

The Barras market

The road leads under a bridge, passing a row of discount shops and Moir Street and Charlotte Street, after which you reach Glasgow's oldest chippie (1884) at Little Dovehill and then Great Dovehill on the left. According to legend, this is where St Mungo was preaching to his flock when someone at the back complained that he could not see him, whereupon he commanded the adjoining ground to rise up in the air.

A little further along is ★ **The Saracen's Head** ⓬ (Saturday 11am–11pm, Sunday 12.30–11pm), or The Sarry Heid, a pub whose glory days are most definitely behind it. It lays claim to being the first real hotel in Glasgow, built in 1755 from the ruins of the old bishop's castle, and takes its name from a 12th-century inn in London frequented by Richard the Lionheart.

The first mail coach from London arrived here in 1788, and it was a haunt of Scotland's judges as they progressed round the western circuit from Edinburgh. It has been visited by an impressive list of patrons, including Robert Burns, John Wesley, James Boswell, William Wordsworth and Adam Smith, who was allegedly ejected after a swearing match with Dr Samuel Johnson.

It houses the 1760 Saracen's Head punchbowl and the skull of Maggie, the last witch to be burned at the stake, which the title deeds demand is to be passed to the People's Palace if the pub is ever demolished.

Bric-a-brac at the Barras

Crossing the road to Kent Street, ★★ **The Barras** ⓭ (every Saturday and Sunday 9am–5pm) originated as a street market consisting of hand-barrows hired out by the McIver family to traders too poor to have their own. The covered market came into being in 1926 and, after a spell in the doldrums in the 1970s and 1980s, it has been revitalised and is now said to be one of the biggest markets in Europe.

Second-hand furniture and clothes predominate, although in keeping with the times, videos, computer games and CDs, whose legality is continually challenged by trading standards officers, now feature. Slightly further along the Gallowgate from the Kent Street entrance is the **Barrowland Ballroom**, a dance hall which was the focus of the 1960s Bible John murders – when three women were killed by a man with a penchant for quoting Old Testament texts to his victims – but is now one of Glasgow's largest live music venues.

Kent Street leads through to London Road, and, turning left, the route passes St Alphonsus Church. Next door is Glasgow Antiques Market (Saturday and Sunday 9.30am–4.30pm) with a café. Proceed down Bain Street, through the Maggie McIvers Gate into Glasgow Green. Turn left for the ★★ **People's Palace** ⓮ (Monday to Thursday and Saturday 10am–5pm, Friday and Sunday 11am–5pm). Through the trees is the exotic coloured-brick frontage of the old **Templeton's carpet factory**, an enthusiastic copy of the Doge's Palace in Venice, designed by William Leiper in 1889. The factory is now a business centre with an excellent bar.

The People's Palace is a museum presiding over one of the tree-lined avenues of Glasgow Green and is a

Templeton's carpet factory

favourite with Glaswegians. It was built as a cultural centre for workers in 1898 and has concentrated on the history and the way of life of the working class as well as kings and cardinals. Exhibits range from a ring which belonged to Mary Queen of Scots to comedian Billy Connolly's 'banana boots'. The red-sandstone building, with its domed roof and pillared frontage, was completely refurbished for its centenary in 1998 and now uses the latest computer technology and film to tell its story. **The Winter Gardens** (daily 10am–5pm), a huge conservatory housing tropical palms and ferns, butts onto the back of the Palace. After a serious fire in January 1998, it has now reopened and houses a café/bar.

In 1450 Bishop Turnbull gave the common lands of **Glasgow Green** to the people of the city, although its previously rural vista is now bounded by the high-rise flats of the Gorbals, across the river. Bonnie Prince Charlie mustered his armies here, and the Glasgow Fair, instituted in 1190, is still celebrated in the park in the last fortnight of July. Turning right past the palace, a 144ft (44m) needle erected to commemorate Lord Nelson dominates the western end. Slightly further on, the magnificent red-terracotta ★ **Doulton Fountain ⑮**, gifted by the Victorian china manufacturer, has recently been restored.

St Andrew's Parish Church, facade detail

Returning north to London Road, along Charlotte Street, you will find Glickman's fabulous confectionery shop (est. 1903), a sweet-tooth's paradise. The route now continues towards Glasgow Cross and then left into James Morrison Street and St Andrew's Square, which houses ★ **St Andrew's Parish Church ⑯** (now known as St Andrew's in the Square), the oldest church in the city after the Cathedral. It was modelled on St Martin's-in-the Fields in London, and its massive pillars and stone ornamentation illustrate the grand tastes of the 18th-century Tobacco Lords. It now has a jazz café in the basement. Across the road is the **Glasgow Police Museum** (summer Monday to Saturday 10am–4.30pm, Sunday noon–4.30pm; winter Tuesday and Sunday, same hours). The museum gives a historical insight into Britain's first police force.

Recalling the first Glasgow bank

The south side of the square passes the district courts, where minor offenders are daily chastised, and, turning left and then right into Steel Street, the route leads to the Saltmarket. The pub on the facing corner, the Old Shipbank, recalls the first Glasgow bank, set up in 1750 to meet the needs of the influential and rising merchant class. Going left down the Saltmarket, the new **High Court of Justiciary** extension is tucked into Jocelyn Square behind the old Mortuary. Further along is the old High Court, with its forbidding grey-pillared portico, which has seen the black cap donned for a procession of murderers. It fronted

The High Court of Justiciary

Central Mosque: the muezzin

The Citizens Theatre
College of Nautical Studies

onto Jail Square, where the guilty were hanged before cheering crowds in the shadow of Nelson's Pillar, giving rise to the maternal Glaswegian warning to recalcitrant children: 'You'll die facing the monument.'

Saltmarket runs down onto the **Albert Bridge**, or Hutchesontown Bridge, a cast-iron structure built in 1871 on enormous granite piers on the site of a crossing first created in 1794. Just upstream is the weir which marks the tidal limit of the river and controls its natural vagaries. Over the bridge, appropriately at the river's junction with the sea, is the **Glasgow College of Nautical Studies**, festooned with lifeboats, survival craft, radar and masts.

Turning right onto the south bank of the river at the start of the college, a tree-lined walkway leads to the peaceful colonnaded grounds of the ★★ **Central Mosque** ⓱ (daily 9am–5pm for visitors, booking essential; 24 hours for prayers), which in 1984 became the first purpose-built mosque in Scotland and is now one of the largest in Europe. Its green, multi-faceted dome and soaring minaret contrast with the 1960s architecture of the surrounding Gorbals. It provides the facilities of worship for 2,000 Muslims, a community whose numbers have increased dramatically in the 1980s and 1990s and who now play an integral part in city life.

The forbidding black-and-grey-marbled building on the other side of Gorbals Street is the ★ **Sheriff Court** ⓲, where solicitors gather to ply an ancient trade that shows no signs of running out of custom. It moved here when the old, smaller, city-centre court became unable to cope with the sheer volume of villains that makes it the busiest court in Europe.

Further south down Gorbals Street, across the junction with Ballater Street, is the ★★ **Citizens Theatre** ⓳ (tel: 0141 429 0022), a cornerstone of Glasgow's artistic life and a major contributor to its ambition to be considered as a European city. It raised its curtain in 1945 in the Princess's Theatre in a row of Gorbals tenements, largely through the efforts of Scottish playwright James Bridie, as part of a plan to establish a Scottish national theatre. But it drifted from drama into crisis until the arrival in 1969 of director Giles Havergal and his flamboyant designer Philip Prowse. Their ground-breaking productions – sometimes shocking and disturbing – attracted headlines and interest far beyond Glasgow and continue to fill the hall. The theatre houses a main auditorium and two small studio theatres which offer cutting-edge works.

Returning along Gorbals Street, the road comes to **Victoria Bridge**, where the city's first river crossing, a wooden structure commissioned by Bishop Rae in 1350, stood for 450 years. The present bridge is faced with Dublin granite and affords excellent views downriver past the Carlton Place Suspension Bridge to the Jamaica Street and Central Station bridges. The Gothic-spired building on the north bank is St Andrew's Cathedral, the main Roman Catholic church, which is reflected in the modern glass-walled diocesan headquarters next door. The glass pyramids rising above the rooftops behind it are the canopies of the St Enoch shopping centre.

Focus of folk: the Clutha Vaults

Across the bridge on the north bank, the two pubs on the right, the **Clutha Vaults** and the **Scotch Corner** (both 11am–midnight), look unappetising from the outside but are a focus for the folk circuit, along with the Scotia Bar in nearby Stockwell Street. They lie on the Clyde Walkway, a riverside promenade, which is steadily reviving the fortunes of a long depressed riverfront with new hotels and apartments.

Above these pubs is the three-tiered spire of the old fish market, topped with a golden sailing ship. It now houses Glasgow Sculpture Studios (GSS), a large studio and workshop space. Veering right into the Bridgegate, or Briggait, one of Glasgow's oldest streets, the route passes second-hand shops and cheap restaurants and the expanse of the King Street car park. Under the railway bridge on waste ground between St Margaret's Place and the new High Court buildings, **Paddy's Market** is held. This is the bottom end of the retail spectrum, with clothes and cast-offs laid out on the ground. It had its origins, as the name suggests, in the floods of refugees from the Irish potato famine, and on market days it can seem that conditions have not greatly improved.

Turning left at the end of the Briggait, the **Saltmarket** – so named because the original market for salt for curing river salmon was sited here – curves back up to the High Street past restored tenements and busy shops.

A lampost decorated with Glasgow's coat of arms

Route 3

The Merchant City

Tron Theatre – Fruitmarket – Ramshorn Kirk – Hutchesons' Hall – Italian Centre – Trades Hall *See map, pages 14–15*

While other cities wrestled with inner-city problems, Glasgow perversely had an outer-city problem. Huge schemes – Drumchapel, Easterhouse, Castlemilk and Pollok, which were created after World War II to facilitate slum clearance – stand guard at each corner of the boundaries. In the late 1970s and early 1980s, Glasgow was tagged Doughnut City – plenty round the outside and nothing in the middle. The Merchant City was Glasgow's attempt to bring life back to the central warehouse district and, by a combination of public and private finance, persuaded developers to convert old buildings into homes in the hope that the necessary baggage of pubs, restaurants and entertainments would follow.

It has been relatively successful. It is not Amsterdam or Paris by a long chalk, but the square-mile area is now home to a core of young professionals who create their own social momentum. The blend of old and new architecture creates an exciting fusion which is echoed in the many restaurants offering innovative cross-cultural food. A new festival venue and a wealth of lively pubs ensure that the nightlife here has a distinctive buzz.

Tron Theatre

Starting the route at the old heart of the city at **Mercat Cross** *(see page 16)*, go west along the Trongate. The tenements along each side date from the middle and end of the 19th century, and their rich facades funnel the street along to an almost Central European steeple whose base is an open arch across the busy pavement. This is **Tron-St Mary's**, a former church, and, like the street, is named after the weighing machine, or tron, introduced by the Bishop of Glasgow in 1491 to weigh and tax goods coming into the city. The church has been operating as the ★ **Tron Theatre** **20** (tel: 0141 552 4267; www.tron.co.uk) since 1982, first as a club and since 1990 as a full public venue. It is a comfortably sized of theatre which features modern as well as traditional Scottish drama, and its restaurant is a popular lunchtime meeting place.

Crossing Trongate from the arches of the church, the route heads up Albion Street, past a magnificent red-sandstone bas-relief on the Cultural and Leisure Services building on the right, to the junction with Bell Street, where a person with a thirst will not long go unsatisfied. This intersection has more pubs than the rest of both long streets put together. On the left, **Blackfriars** is large and lively, with a basement which hosts live music nights; **Café Gandolfi**, on the right, was one of the original Merchant City restaurants and contains the fantastical wood furniture of Tim Stead. **Gandolfi Fish**, an excellent seafood haunt, is just a few doors along. Nearby, **Bargo** was converted from an old cheese market and features comfortable sofas; across the road is the huge O'Neill's pub, at the south end of the ★ **Old Fruit Market ㉑**.

Minimalism in Bargo

The fruitmarket moved from its congested home here in 1969 and now nestles, with the fishmarket, beside the M8 at Blochairn. The south end housed a successful general market for many years before closing to accommodate the above-mentioned pub. The north end, however, lay closed for years, until enthusiasts from the performing arts section of the council realised that its cobbled streets and balconied offices, which used to ring to the iron wheels of carts and the shouts of traders, would make an ideal, New Orleans-style venue for the annual **Glasgow Jazz Festival**. The extensively refurbished Old Fruitmarket is a much-loved performance space and hosts regular events and parties.

The building above the Italian Kitchen (pizzeria and café), where Albion Street crosses Ingram Street, housed the original Mitchell Library collection on two floors in 1877. Stephen Mitchell came from a tobacco family and left a huge estate to provide books 'on all subjects not immoral' for the edification of the city's working classes. His initiative was the impetus for the public library service, and the present Mitchell Library *(see page 36)* is the largest public reference library in Europe.

On the opposite corner, Greenwich Village-style loft apartments are situated in a former Strathclyde University building. Further up Albion Street, the four-storey black-glass office formerly housed *The Herald* newspaper, which

Wood furniture in Café Gandolfi

prides itself on being the world's oldest English-language daily. The newspaper has moved to offices in the city centre and the old offices are to be turned into flats. The open space opposite is to house a new city science park and possibly a new hotel.

Looking right along Ingram Street, the **Ad Lib** bar/diner (tel: 0141 552 2929) on the right hand side is housed in a red-sandstone building with a splendid coat of arms over the entrance. This was the Central Fire Station, built in 1899, and the home of Wallace the Fire Dog, the mascot who faithfully escorted the engines on their dangerous missions. The engine room used to contain a memorial to the 19 firemen who died in the Cheapside Street whisky bond blaze in 1960, an event which still scars the memory of many families in the city.

As you turn left along Ingram Street, the ★ **Ramshorn Kirk** ㉒ looms out of a grove of unlikely urban elms. The Gothic church with its square clock tower is properly known as St David's (Ramshorn) and was built in 1824 on the Ramshorn estate. It is tall and narrow, with soaring stained-glass windows, and houses a substantial crypt. The building is now used by the Strathclyde University Theatre Group, which stages an eclectic repertoire in the small performance space (see local press for details) and uses the crypt as rehearsal rooms.

The **Ramshorn Cemetery** is a verdant respite from street noise and a fascinating voice from the past. Many gravestones are so old as to be illegible, and some are still barred and spiked against the predations of graver-obbers. Emile L'Angelier, arsenic victim of the infamous Madeleine Smith, is buried here, as is David Dale, phil-anthropic co-founder of New Lanark, and John 'Phos-phoros' Anderson, the ebullient father of Strathclyde University. On the pavement outside, worn by thousands of careless feet, are the initials R.F. and A.F., marking the resting place of the Foulis brothers, a pair of enter-prising and painstaking printers who perfected the craft for Glasgow University in the 18th century. Robert Foulis was also instrumental in establishing an Academy of Arts some 14 years before the Royal Academy in London.

The Ramshorn Kirk and Cemetery

The Ramshorn stands sentinel at the head of **Candle-riggs**, a street which takes its name from the noisome candleworks which initially operated well away from the main population. This is the heart of the Merchant City, with coffee houses and fashionable bars on the right and the substantially refurbished ★ **City Halls** ㉓, where Dickens drew crowds for his readings and where every hue of political opinion has been heard, on the left. When the halls were built in 1841, they could accommodate an as-tonishing 3,500 people.

The City Halls

Further down on the left, the pavement outside the City Halls has interesting marblework, created when the street cobbles were renewed and which reflects the area's age:

Ghostly workers sleep below,
They hear no rain or heel and toe,
Think of them where the forges glow,
In the Glasgow of long ago.

Turning right into Wilson Street, new apartment buildings blend with the imposing bulk of the old warehouse district and smart design shops nestle below. Continuing right into Brunswick Street, a sandstone Victorian building with huge Ionic columns occupies the entire block. This was the old ★ **Glasgow Sheriff Court** ㉔, which opened in 1892 and closed in 1984, having witnessed nearly a century of unmitigated villainy. It once housed a whipping table (now in Strathclyde Police's Black Museum in Pitt Street) and was said to be haunted by a lady in white.

The old Glasgow Sheriff Court

29

The building is currently being used as the home of the Scottish Youth Theatre, a retail complex and smart residential apartments.

Passing the **Brunswick Hotel** on the right, the flats at the corner of Brunswick Street and Ingram Street are a fine example of facade retention. The site was originally the warehouse premises of Campbell, Stewart & McDonald, and was one of the first in the Merchant City to tear out and replace the whole interior while keeping the architecturally important shell. The same thing is now happening with new district council buildings across the road.

The white building on the opposite side of Ingram Street is ★★ **Hutchesons' Hall** ㉕ (irregular opening hours; contact NTS on 0844 493 2134 for the latest hours). Statues of George and Thomas Hutcheson, brothers from a

Al fresco on Candleriggs

Hutchesons' Hall

landowning family, peer down from niches in the classical front. They, like many Glasgow businessmen, were of a philanthropic bent, and on his death in 1639 Thomas made provision for a hospital for 12 'poore decrippet men'. George added more funds on his death two years later.

The hospital was originally in the Trongate, and moved to its present location in 1806 to a design by David Hamilton, with further reconstruction work by John Baird in 1876. The interior is quite simply stunning. It was acquired in 1982 by the National Trust for Scotland – visit their website: www.nts.org.uk – whose renovations have been scrupulous and sympathetic. The Trust runs a shop and information room which contains material relating to the Merchant City Trail.

Just past Hutcheson's Hall is the busy pedestrianised concourse of the ★★ **Italian Centre** ㉖ in John Street. In this short stretch, on a sunny summer day, Glasgow can consider itself to be a European city. White-aproned waiters rush back and forth to tables of animated diners talking on their mobiles below the restaurants' canopies. A bronze of Mercury keeps an eye on the shoppers with their Armani and Versace bags, and the view up through the arches of the City Chambers *(see pages 31–2)* is a symphony in stone.

Leaving the Italian Centre, the squat domed building on the corner of Glassford Street houses a retail outlet. The building was designed by John Burnet and is a splendid example of late-Victorian confidence. Slightly further down on the same side is the ★★ **Trades Hall** ㉗ (Monday to Friday 9am–5pm, Saturday 9am–noon; self-guided audio tours available; tel: 0141 552 2418), which well-worn tradition dictates is, apart from the Cathedral, the oldest building in the city which still fulfils its original function. It is the home of the 14 trades of Glasgow, which include hammermen, fleshers, bonnetmakers, weavers and barbers (who were the early surgeons), and their symbol – 14 arrows bound together – adorns the magnificent curving staircase which leads into the grand hall. The hall is lined with a magnificent mirrored silk frieze – the 3-D of its time – showing the trades about their business.

The Trades Hall is also the home of the Trades House, whose business these days is mainly philanthropic – it dispenses more than £1 million a year in charity. It is worth a visit, especially for the benches carved by Belgian refugees in the entranceway, the Adam plasterwork and wood ceilings, and the *kists*, or chests, which are opened only once a year and contain a time capsule of trinkets dating back to 1604.

Return to Glasgow Cross by following Glassford Street south and turning left into Argyle Street.

Trades Hall: the banqueting hall

... and silk frieze detail

Route 4

Inside the City Chambers

The City Centre

George Square – City Chambers – Gallery of Modern Art – Stock Exchange Building – Buchanan Street – Merchants' House *See map, pages 14–15*

This walk presents a minor dilemma. Some will tell you to look up, to see the wealth of mighty stonework of these urban canyons. Others say keep a watch at pavement level to see the lunchtime crowds practise the old sport of aggressive jaywalking. Wherever you look, this is a busy part of the city.

Queen Street Station, our starting point, runs frequent railway services to Edinburgh and all points north, as well as a suburban service from the Clyde coast to Lanarkshire *(see page 73)*. Built on the site of a quarry in 1842 with a daring curved glass roof, it is Glasgow's oldest station. Beside it, ★★ **George Square** ㉘ began as a muddy hollow in 1781 and developed into a civic meeting place over two centuries. Its beautiful lawns have been replaced with red tarmac, much to the chagrin of office workers who sunbathed there at the first blink of sunshine.

George Square statue

The **Millennium Hotel** to the right of the station as you face it was, naturally, a railway hotel, and the BR initials can still be seen above the doorway. It was at a dinner here in 1941 that Roosevelt's World War II envoy Harry Hopkins pledged American support to Britain against Hitler with the biblical reply: 'Whither thou goest, I will go; and where thou lodgest, I will lodge; thy people shall be my people, and thy God my God.' Winston Churchill broke down in tears.

The next office block on the left is best sped past in order to come to the ★★★ **City Chambers** ㉙ (Ground

The marble staircase

St Vincent Place

Floor only, Monday to Friday 8.30am–5pm; guided tours of whole building, Monday to Friday 10.30am and 2.30pm), the towering statement of Glasgow's Victorian confidence on the east side of the square. It was opened in 1888 and, according to the architect, was a 'free treatment of the Italian Renaissance'. The ornate front has witnessed momentous events in the square below, including the raising of the hammer and sickle by the Glasgow Soviet in 1919.

The interiors are a riot of marble, mosaic and alabaster. The vaulted ceiling of the entrance hall alone is covered with one and a half million Venetian mosaic tiles. Granite and marble staircases lead like Escher paintings to the council chambers where the Lord Provost presides over the city's affairs. Civic functions are regularly held in the great Banqueting Hall, under murals painted by 'Glasgow Boys' Henry, Lavery and Roche portraying the city's colourful history.

Passing the white, lion-flanked monolith of the **Cenotaph**, the south side of the square begins with the former General Post Office which is being developed as luxury town flats. Across Hanover Street, the middle office on the block is that of the ★ **Glasgow Tourist Office 30** (tel: 0141 204 4400, May to June and September, Monday to Saturday 9am–7pm, Sunday 10am– 6pm; July and August, Monday to Saturday 9am–8pm, Sunday 10am–6pm; April to October, Monday to Saturday 9am–6pm; www.seeglasgow.com).

Turning left down Queen Street, past bars and fast-food restaurants, the great pillared hall on the right in Royal Exchange Square is the ★★ **Gallery of Modern Art 31** (tel: 0141 229 1996, Monday to Wednesday and Saturday 10am–5pm, Thursday 10am–8pm, Friday and Sunday 11am–5pm). Guarded by a statue of Wellington by Baron Marocchetti (which revellers grace most Friday and Saturday nights with a traffic cone), the gallery was previously the Stirling Library. It grew out of a house, owned by tobacco baron William Cunningham of Lainshaw, and the huge Corinthian columns at the front and the hall at the rear were added later. The gallery opened in a welter of controversy about its collection. Many critics damned it for populism, but the citizens voted with their feet, and attendances continue to exceed expectations. It is divided into four galleries, with exhibits from the New Glasgow Boys – Howson, Campbell, Wisnieski and Currie – much in evidence. The upper galleries use natural light wonderfully, and recent exhibitions have featured the dramatic works of David Mach. There is a small café in the basement by the Martyr's Library.

Returning up Queen Street and turning left, ★ **St Vincent Place 32** opens up an august street of banks and offices faced with the full repertoire of the Victorian mason's craft.

The Clydesdale Bank on the north side has bas-reliefs, crouching men and encircled emblems of the towns where the bank has had a presence. Opposite, the Scottish Provident Building's red sandstone reaches skyward.

However, not all these structures are devoted to serious purpose: **The Counting House** (tel: 0141 225 0160) on the corner of George Square has been converted into a pub and restaurant with splendid interior statuary, cornicing and glass dome above the bar; **The Auctioneers** (tel: 0141 229 5851) in North Court is also a pub and restaurant furbished with the kind of bric-a-brac which used to pass through McTear's showrooms, and **78 St Vincent** (tel: 0141 248 7878) is beautifully lit by the vaulting windows of a former bank, and has an interior reminiscent of Le Chartier restaurant in Paris.

The Auctioneers

Passing a variety of city shops on the left, the route turns right into West Nile Street and right again into West George Street. The church in the centre of the road is ★ **St George's Tron** ㉝, built in 1807 to accommodate the westward movement of the city. It was designed by William Stark, who was also responsible for a jail on Glasgow Green and a lunatic asylum. On the north side of the square, Nelson Mandela Place, is the former Old Athenaeum which, on opening in 1888, offered classes in science, philosophy and literature to more than 1,000 students. It now houses shops and restaurants. Tucked into the corner is the Royal Faculty of Procurators Hall, with the heads of law lords carved on the window arches.

33

Stock Exchange detail

On the other side of the square is the early French Gothic extravagance of the former ★ **Glasgow Stock Exchange** building ㉞, which recalls the London Law Courts and is a rare flight of fancy amid the solidity of its surroundings. It, too, is now shops. The wide avenue of

78 St Vincent

Princes Square

Rogano for shellfish

Merchants' House details

★★ **Buchanan Street** ③⑤, the city's most prestigious shopping arena, stretches southward. It starts at Argyle Street, with Frasers on its domed corner site, and leads up a Victorian canyon fronted by designer names. In the pedestrianised centre is the winged *Spirit of St Kentigern* statue, and buskers, from lone, dowdy evangelists to full string quartets, provide daily entertainment.

Further along on the right is the Argyll Arcade, an enclosed walkway lined with jewellers' shops, which rightangles back to Argyle Street. Nearby is the entrance to ★★★ **Princes Square** ③⑥, a beautiful mall packed with trendy boutiques and bars on several levels. It is best entered via the central escalator, past the *trompe l'oeil* paintings of worthies like Sir Thomas Lipton, Keir Hardie and John Logie Baird.

On the top floor while looking down at the mosaic of the central well, you will not be able to help noticing the huge **Foucalt's Pendulum**, a replica of the device by which Jean Bernard Léon Foucalt proved the rotation of the Earth in the dome of the Pantheon in Paris in 1851. The centre is a shopaholic's dream, with the presence of top names in fashion such as Calvin Klein and Ted Baker.

Back on Buchanan Street, the shopping choice is wide, from the Hugo Boss store on the left to Russell & Bromley and L'Occitane on the right or the new multi-level **Borders Books** bookstore in the old Royal Bank building opposite Gordon Street. The new Apple computer store is one of Buchanan Street's latest offerings. Wearied shoppers can stop at the Mackintosh **Willow Tea Rooms** *(see page 49)*, a replica based on the many remnants owned by the City Council, or ★ **Rogano** ③⑦, a splendid art deco shellfish restaurant situated in the passageway leading to Royal Exchange Square.

Past Graham Tiso, Hobbs and The White Company and back across St Vincent Street to the Stock Exchange, the view north takes in the ★ **Buchanan Galleries** ③⑧, an enormous shopping complex development which encompasses several city blocks and a pedestrianised area at the ★ **Glasgow Royal Concert Hall** ③⑨ (tel: 0141 353 8000; www.grch.com), the main venue for classical concerts. The centrepiece here is a statue of the late Donald Dewar, credited as the driving force behind the new Scottish Parliament.

Returning along West George Street to George Square, the oriel-windowed ★★ **Merchants' House** ④⓪ (Monday to Thursday 9am–12.30pm, subject to functions) reflects the confidence and self-importance of the guilds which created it. Housing the Chamber of Commerce, which is the second-oldest in the world after that of New York, it hosts occasional concerts (see local press for details).

Going West

St Vincent Street Church – The King's Theatre – Mitchell Library – Tenement House – St Aloysius Church *See map, pages 14–15*

The city has been moving west since medieval times, and, since the more prosperous were the first to decamp, the buildings become noticeably more ornate. Starting the route at the junction of Hope Street and St Vincent Street, the Victorian offices spiral upwards in ever more detailed flights of the stonemason's fancy. Looking south, the clock tower of the Central Hotel looms above Central Station, the main link to the south, in austere welcome.

St Vincent Street, named after the naval battle at Cabo de São Vicente, is a thoroughfare devoted to Mammon, so it is fitting that its long incline is crowned with one of Scotland's finest temples to God. ★★ **St Vincent Street Free Church of Scotland ❹** is the best remaining example of the work of Alexander 'Greek' Thomson (1817–75). Thomson, para-doxically, is famous for being Glasgow's 'forgotten archi-tect', forever in the shadow of Charles Rennie Mackintosh *(see pages 48–49)*. Like Mackintosh, he wanted to design every detail of a commission, down to the decorations on the walls. This is the only one of his three city churches still intact, and it has been added to the World Monument Watch for endangered buildings. Light from enormous windows bathes the sumptuous interior, and a recently repaired tower, which recalls India rather than Greece, dominates Blythswood Hill.

The Free Church of Scotland and detail

35

On the right, slightly further down the hill, the needle spire of ★ **St Columba's Gaelic Church** soars heaven-wards. It has its roots in the influx of Highlanders who flocked to the city after the Clearances, when landlords evicted crofters to make way for sheep.

The western end of St Vincent Street is enveloped by the roar of the traffic on the M8, which cuts through an underpass on its way to Edinburgh. The marble and mir-rored glass tower on the left is the **Hilton International ❷**, which has become one of the city's most prestigious venues. Inside, ★ **Cameron's** restaurant specialises in fresh Scottish produce.

Turning right into Elmbank Street, the white building on the right is the former **High School**, with its statues of Galileo, Cicero, Homer and James Watt. The school dates back to the 15th century, but it has gradually moved west from its original home and is now situated in more space in Anniesland. Today, the buildings are occupied by

The former High School

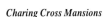

council offices. On the corner of Elmbank Crescent, the ornate grey-stone building provides the rehearsal rooms for Scottish Opera and Scottish Ballet, two of Scotland's most prestigious companies. It used to be the home of the Institute of Shipbuilders and Engineers, and a bronze plaque just inside the entrance pays tribute to the engineers who went down at their posts on the *Titanic* in 1912.

★ **The King's Theatre ❸** (tel: 0141 240 1111), on the corner of Elmbank Street and Bath Street, was the most fashionable Glasgow venue of the Edwardian age. Built in 1904, with a lion mascot in stone above the entrance, it provides a stage for a variety of shows. The **Griffin Bar** opposite dates from the same period.

Mitchell Library

Heading left down Bath Street through a canyon of modern offices, the splendid dome of the ★★ **Mitchell Library ❹** (Monday to Thursday 9am–8pm, Friday and Saturday 9am–5pm, closed Sunday) with its statue of Minerva rises above the motorway traffic. It was the legacy of tobacco heir Stephen Mitchell, and, after homes in Ingram Street and Miller Street, the collection moved to the present site in 1911. It is now the biggest public reference library in Europe, and its comprehensive Glasgow Room is a boon and a blessing to those with an interest in the city.

36

Charing Cross Mansions

Up North Street and across Sauchiehall Street, the ornate fountain at **Charing Cross** may not have the cachet of Pisa, but the drunken angle at which it leans is every bit as dramatic. Walking north, head for the **pedestrian bridge** which spans the motorway. A pause here affords a close-up look at the graceful red-sandstone curve of Charing Cross Mansions and, on the left, the turrets, arched windows and balconies of St George's Mansions, both testament to the graciousness into which tenement living evolved.

The Tenement House

It pays to keep this Edwardian splendour in mind on the walk from the end of the bridge on the path up through grass and trees to ★★ **The Tenement House ❺** (March to October daily 1pm–5pm, last admissions 4.30pm). It lies at the end of the walkway at 145 Buccleuch Street and is fascinating not because it is special, but because it was so typical. It was the home for 50 years of a spinster who changed nothing in her 'wally close' (tiled common stairway). The gaslit parlour and the black range – and the rosewood piano – are, as the National Trust for Scotland which now runs it says, 'a sure sign of gentility'.

Returning along Buccleuch Street, right into Garnethill Street and left into Hill Street, this was for many years the heart of the ethnic Chinese community. On the other side, Italy is recalled by the domed grandeur of **St Aloysius Church**, which is attached to the Jesuit school further up the street.

Route 6

Statue in Kelvingrove Park

Parks and Galleries

Woodlands Road – Park Circus – Kelvingrove Park – Art Gallery and Museum – Kelvin Hall – Museum of Transport *See map, page 38*

Glasgow is peppered with bronze memorials of the cream of Victoria's empire, but the statue which holds the fondest place in the hearts of Glaswegians is of a mustachioed sheriff astride a two-legged horse. It is to be found at the start of this walk on the corner of Woodlands Road, which runs west from Charing Cross *(see page 36)* and Park Drive.

Lobey Dosser

★ **Lobey Dosser** ㊻, as the statue is called, was the creation of a newspaper cartoonist called Bud Neill who, more than anyone before or since, captured the sharp but skewed sense of the city's humour. Regulars in the **Halt Bar** across the road were instrumental in raising the public subscription in 1992 to the memory of the Sheriff of Calton Creek and his masked adversary Rank Bajin. The question 'What was the name of Lobey Dosser's horse?' has sparked a thousand pub arguments, and knowing the answer (El Fideldo) will give you instant credibility with Glaswegians.

Leaving the mix of antique shops and restaurants in Woodlands Road, the route runs from the spire of St Jude's Free Presbyterian Church up through the greenery of Woodlands Hill and left into Lynedoch Place. This wide street leads to an area of flats and offices dominated by the Italianate towers of ★ **Trinity College** ㊼, formerly the college of the Free Church and now much sought-after flats. Along with the lonely white tower of the Park Parish Church – the rest of it was demolished in the late 1960s – they form a dramatic focus of the city skyline.

Trinity College

Park Circus

Earl Roberts of Kandahar

Turn right into Park Circus Place and enter the splendid oval of ★ **Park Circus** ㊽, with its air of Victorian elegance. The grand curving terraces rising to a bluff above the River Kelvin were designed as private housing for the emergent middle classes by Charles Wilson (1810–63) and can justly be regarded as his masterpiece.

They lead to ★★ **Kelvingrove Park** ㊾, the first custom-built park in the city and the site of three great International Exhibitions, in 1888, 1901 and 1911, which proudly proclaimed Glasgow's contribution to the British Empire. This entrance is guarded by a spectacular statue of Field Marshal Earl Roberts of Kandahar (1832–1914), surrounded by the bas-relief trappings of his Indian campaigns. There is a similar statue of the field marshal in Calcutta. The park itself is a fine example of the ornamental pleasure garden, with winding paths and wide boulevards. Descending into the park, the main thoroughfare and bridge are marked by a memorial to the officers and men of the Highland Light Infantry who fell in the 'South African War' or Boer War (1899–1902). Turning left here, the road leads through dappled shade to the extravagance of the ★ **Stewart Memorial Fountain** ㊿, a tribute to the Lord Provost who, in 1855, finally managed to secure a supply of pure water to the city from Loch Katrine in the Trossachs.

Turning right past the skateboard park and the duck ponds, the route emerges onto the Kelvin Way, and a bridge cornered by four groups of bronzes representing peace and war, commerce and industry, shipping and navigation, and prosperity and progress. They were badly damaged by German bombers in 1941 and restored by sculptor Benno Schotz 10 years later.

The path opposite the park gate leads to the red-sandstone grandeur of ★★★ **Kelvingrove Art Gallery and Museum** **51** (Monday to Thursday and Saturday 10am–5pm, Friday and Sunday 11am–5pm; tel: 0141 276 9599; free guided tours), a superb repository of one of the finest civic collections in Europe. The gallery had its origins in the paintings of Trades House Deacon Convenor Archibald McLellan, which the city acquired in 1854 along with his gallery in Sauchiehall Street. The need to house these and other displays led to the 1888 Exhibition – a mammoth event attended by Queen Victoria and nearly 6 million of her subjects – and the profits were used as pump-priming money for the new building.

Kelvingrove Art Gallery and Museum

The project was conceived on a breathtaking scale, with its twin towers, which shelter a massive bronze of St Mungo, facing the lacework spire of Glasgow University, and the other side leading down a grand staircase onto sunken gardens. Visited by over 1 million people each year, in 2007 the Kelvingrove reopened its impressive interior after a £27.9 million, three-year refurbishment. Its huge galleries are arranged around two naturally lit halls on either side of the Great Hall which has an immense Lewis pipe organ still used for recitals.

Elvis points the way at the Kelvingrove

The collection, which includes over 8,000 objects, over three floors and many interactive displays, also features many 17th-century Dutch and French Impressionist and post-Impressionist paintings. Rembrandt's *Man in Armour*, Millet's *Going to Work* and Dalí's *Christ of St John of the Cross* are particular favourites. The Glasgow School, in the forefront of the departure from classical tradition, and the Scottish Colourists are well represented, and among the 3,000 oils and 12,500 drawings and prints are works by Rubens, Pissarro, Van Gogh, Degas, Matisse and Monet. Within the walls of this cultural treasure trove, visitors to the West Wing will find a WWII Spitfire hanging from the ceiling.

A WWII Spitfire hangs from the ceiling

Leaving from the west end of the art gallery, past the 'machine-gun Tommy' war memorial, cross the street to the ★ **Kelvin Hall** (tel: 0141 357 2525), which for many years was Glasgow's foremost exhibition centre, and is fondly remembered for the annual carnival and circus, complete with elephants and their distinctive aroma. Built in 1927, it served for 60 years – including war service as a

Cars for connoisseurs at the Museum of Transport

Kelvin Hall logo

Transport Museum exhibit

barrage balloon factory – before its functions were transferred to the Scottish Exhibition and Conference Centre next to the Clyde.

It now serves two functions. The front entrance is to the ★ **International Sports Centre ➄** (Sunday to Tuesday and Thursday to Friday 9am–10.30pm, Wednesday 10am–10.30pm, last booking 9.30pm, Saturday 9am–6.30pm, last booking 5.30pm), which has an international standard running track that can hold 5,000 spectators. Two other halls offer every type of sport. Round the corner in Bunhouse Road is another entrance, which leads to the ★★ **Museum of Transport ➄** (Monday to Thursday and Saturday 10am–5pm, Friday and Sunday 11am–5pm), a fascinating collection ranging from motorcycles and fire engines to tramcars, full-sized locomotives and steam and motor cars. It has the world's finest assembly of Scottish-built cars, including Albions, Arrol-Johnstons, Beardmores and Argylls. By 2011 the Museum of Transport will relocate to a new multi-million pound riverside museum planned for construction on the banks of the River Clyde.

The Clyde Room is a tribute to the shipbuilding tradition, with a comprehensive selection of models of warships, ocean liners and merchantmen which were launched into the muddy waters of the river. Many were presentation pieces at the launch – like the *Queen Mary* and the two *Queen Elizabeths* – and the detail and craftsmanship is a joy. The museum also has a life-sized replica street from 1938, including shops and a cinema, which on a Saturday shows children's films.

Frequent bus services on Dumbarton Road return to the city centre, but first it is worth a quick look downriver at the **Bishop's Mill**, with its distinctive wheatsheaf finials. It sits on a natural weir, and the site has been used since the 12th century. It has now been converted for housing.

Route 7

The West End

Kelvin Way – Glasgow University – Hunterian Museum – Hunterian Art Gallery – The Lanes – Byres Road – Botanic Gardens *See map, page 38*

In the hungry 1930s, the young Turks of Govan would cross on the Kelvinhaugh Ferry of a Sunday afternoon and stage their own version of the Latin *paseo* (walking out) with the local girls along the bosky grandeur of the Kelvin Way. And to the boys from the shipyard tenements it must have seemed like a foreign country. This is a lovely walk.

Starting at the Sauchiehall Street end of the **Kelvin Way**, the Art Galleries open up on the left and the imposing Gothic front of Glasgow University looms on Gilmorehill. Mature trees canopy the Way after it crosses the bridge with its four dramatic bronzes by Paul R. Montford. On the right is the Kelvingrove bandstand, now sadly derelict (although a restoration is planned), and, by an azalea-studded rockery further along on the left, sit the figures of the great scientist Lord Kelvin (1824–1907) and surgery pioneer Joseph Lister (1827–1912), both in their university robes.

Kelvin Way and Lord Kelvin

41

At the end is a cluster of university buildings, with the imposing gothic **Glasgow University Union** straight ahead and the Gilmorehill Centre in a former church on the right. Turning left onto the hill of University Avenue is the gilded gatehouse of ★ **Pearce Lodge** 54, a remnant of the 17th-century Old College in the city centre, which until recently housed the very 21st-century Computing Service.

Up the hill on the right is the ★ **Wellington Church** 55, a grand classical structure influenced by the Madeleine in Paris, with 10 massive fluted pillars supporting its portico. Its predecessor stood in Wellington Street in the centre of the city and attracted a well-to-do congregation, evidenced by the fact that its war memorial lists mainly officers, with only a scatter of enlisted men. There is a small café downstairs in the crypt. Next door is the bright, galleried circle of ★ **The Reading Room** 56, a quirky but practical study area built in the grounds of Hillhead House, given to the university in 1917 in memory of city merchant Walter MacLellan of Rhu.

The Reading Room

★★ **Glasgow University** 57, directly across from the Reading Room, is one of the world's great seats of learning, with an outstanding academic history *(see page 17)* and worldwide influence. It is the fourth-oldest in Britain after St Andrews, Oxford and Cambridge. In 1870 it moved to its current site, a leaded-windowed building designed by Sir John Gilbert Scott in what he called 'a 13th

The University's wrought-iron gate

or 14th century secular style… with Scottish features'. A complex wrought-iron gate which carries the motto *Via Veritas Vita* contains the names of such luminaries as Bute, Kelvin, Lister, Watt, Stair, Adam Smith and Foulis. Just inside is a monument to William and John Hunter, the medical brothers whose collection forms the basis of the newly refurbished Hunterian Museum, and the award-winning ★ **Visitor Centre** ❺❽ (October to April, Monday to Saturday 9.30am–5pm; May to September, Monday to Saturday 9.30am–6pm, Sunday 2pm–5pm) provides comprehensive information with guided tours of the university (May to September, Wednesday–Friday and Saturday 11am and 2pm; October to April, Wednesday 2pm). The Friday tour up the tower has excellent views of the city.

A staircase by the Visitor Centre leads to the sunlit quadrangles and the contrastingly gloomy cloisters. Here also is the lusciously ornate Bute Hall and the ★★ **Hunterian Museum** ❺❾ (Monday to Saturday 9.30am–5pm), Scotland's oldest, which displays the death mask of founder William Hunter. Its splendid galleries house material of great antiquity, from dinosaurs' eggs and rare material from Captain Cook's voyages to ancient coins and a history of the Romans in Scotland. Emerging again by the Visitor Centre and turning left, the route reaches The Square, which houses the Principal's residence and the University Chapel.

Directly across from the university gatehouse is the ★★ **Hunterian Gallery** ❻⓿ (Monday to Saturday 9.30am –5pm) and the Mackintosh House within it *(see page 49)*, with its internationally famous Whistler collection and works by Rembrandt, Pissarro, Sisley and Rodin. The University library is a few steps further up Southpark Avenue.

Abandoning academia for more esoteric pleasures, **Byres Road**, at the junction with University Avenue, presents itself as the students' playground. Named after a

42

The Hunterian Museum

small *clachan*, or village, called Byres of Partick which once stood there, it is a cosmopolitan mix of restaurants, bars and cafés, and comfortingly solid tenement architecture. Kember and Jones, an upmarket deli and café, and The University Café are both excellent eateries on Byres Road. A brief detour up Highburgh Road opposite the junction leads to ★ **Cottiers** ❻❶ (tel: 0141 357 3868), a superb theatre, bar and restaurant in a Victorian Gothic church by architect William Leiper, featuring the beautifully restored stained glass and interior design of Daniel Cottier. It hosts shows by Scottish Opera and Scottish Ballet as well as experimental companies. Jazz is played on Sunday, 5–8pm.

Botanic Gardens

To return to the route, just before University Avenue reaches Byres Road, turn right into Ashton Road and right again into ★ **Ashton Lane** ❻❷. This leads down an alley into an explosion of constantly busy bars and restaurants. In less than 100 yards (90m), this narrow, cobbled lane offers Brel (tel: 0141 342 4966), with Belgian beer and 'rustic' food, Cul de Sac (tel: 0141 334 4749), an eclectic bar and restaurant, the wacky Vodka Wodka, the Grosvenor Cinema, Jinty McGuinty's packed Irish bar, the Ubiquitous Chip (tel: 0141 334 5007) and the Ashoka Indian restaurant (tel: 0141 337 1115). Ruthven Lane close by has antiquarian bookstores and vintage and designer clothes.

43

Going north up Byres Road past Hillhead Underground and Curlers, an old coaching inn, turn right into Great George Street and then left into ★ **Cresswell Lane** ❻❸ for De Courcy's Arcade, a warren of stalls selling linen, jewels, games and records. At the end, turn left and then right again into Byres Road to the junction with Great Western Road. On the right is the pyramid spire of the former Kelvinside Parish Church, which has been converted into the Oranór music centre, restaurant and bar. On the left is the terrace of the **Grosvenor Hotel**, a quarter-mile repetition of the facades of Venetian palaces. The eastern half was destroyed in a fire in 1978 and rebuilt with glass-reinforced concrete cast from the original pillars.

Bright lights in Ashton Lane

Directly opposite are the ★★ **Botanic Gardens** ❻❹ (the Gardens are open from 7am until dusk daily; the Glasshouses 10am–4.45pm, 4.15pm in winter; the Visitor Centre 11am–4pm), a restful recreation garden relocated from Sauchiehall Street to Kelvinside in 1842, with a herb garden, uncommon vegetable garden and walks along the Kelvin. Dramatic glasshouses nurture tropical plants. The delicate dome of the Kibble Palace was brought here from the Clyde coast home of John Kibble in 1873.

Just up Queen Margaret Drive on the right is a building that once used to house the women students of Queen Margaret College. Return to the city centre by bus from Great Western Road or by Underground from Hillhead (Byres Road) or Kelvinbridge (down Great Western Road).

ROUTE 8

GOVAN

River Clyde

Edmiston Drive

Paisley Road West

M8

Craigton Cemetery

Paisley Road West

The Art Lover' House Ⓜ

Bellahouston Park

Mosspark Boulevard

Dumbreck Road

Nithsdale

POLLOKSHIELDS

Kingston St

Morrison St Nelson St

West St Wallace St

Cook St

Ⓜ Scotland Street School

St Andrews Road

St Andrew's Cross

SOUTH CARDONALD

St Andrew's Drive

Harriet Road

Maxwell Park

Terregles Avenue

Darnley Road

Pollokshaws

GOVAN HILL

M77

Titwood Road

White Cart Water

Pollok Country Park **66**

68 Burrell Collection

67 Pollok House

Pollokshaws Road

Queen's Park **65**

Queens Drive

Langside Avenue

Prospect Hill Road

8

Pollok Golf Course

Barrhead Road

Barrhead Road

Victoria Infirmary

Battlefield Road

Clarkson Road

POLLOKSHAWS

COWGLEN

Cowglen Golf Course

Auld Nether Auldhouse Road

House Road

Kilmarnock Road

Newlands Road

Langside Drive

Merrylea Road

8

Thornliebank Road

Fenwick Road

THORNLIEBANK

Braidholm Road

Braidholm Park

Cemetery

White Cart Water

Linn Park → Golf Course

Nitshill Road

M77

Stevenson Road

Rouken Glen Road

69 Rouken Glen Park

Davieland Road

8

Williamwood Golf Course

Eastwoodmains Road

Clarkson Road

Linn Park

Thornliebank Road

Ayr Road

Cathcart Castle Golf Course

Mearns Road

Ⓜ The Mackintosh Tour

Whitecraigs Golf Course

8 **70** Greenbank Garden

0 1000 metres
0 1000 yards

N

Route 8

The South Side

**Queen's Park – Pollok Estate – Burrell Collection –
Rouken Glen – Greenbank Garden** *See map opposite*

A car would be the best means for this tour, since it is not
feasible on foot and public transport would be complicated.

Start from Argyle Street at Jamaica Street *(see map on
pages 14–15)* and, crossing Glasgow Bridge – built in 1899
following a Thomas Telford design – get in the middle lane,
pass the classical tenements of **Carlton Place** to the left
and head south along Eglinton Street. This area was a riverside hinterland for much of the 20th century and still bears
the marks of commerce with warehouses, disused facto-
ries and railway arches. Turn left just before a McDonald's
restaurant at Cuthbertson Street and right into Victoria
Road, a wide avenue of small shops, pubs and restaurants
which leads to the gates of ★ **Queen's Park** ❻.

Carlton Place

Although built in the reign of Victoria, these rolling
grounds take their name from Mary Queen of Scots, whose
supporters lost the Battle of Langside nearby in 1568. The
park rises to an impressive summit, with panoramic views
as far as Ben Lomond in the north and Lanark in the south.
Turning left at the gates, Langside Road, which is not signposted, runs round the park past the **Victoria Infirmary**
– a huge hospital serving the whole of the south side of
Glasgow – to the monument on Battle Place, designed
by Alexander Skirving in 1887, and an imposing stone-
cleaned former church which has been converted to the
Budda bar and restaurant.

Queen's Park **45**

Going straight ahead at the roundabout, follow Millbrae
Road into Langside Drive, turn right at Newlands Road
(you'll see a sign for Diarsie House School) and follow
it to Riverford Road. Go through an area of high-rise flats,
past the high chimney stack of the old Pollokshaws
'Steamie', now a sports centre, and onto Pollokshaws Road
at the 1897 Town Hall. Turn left here, then immediately
right for the entrance to Pollok Estate.

These beautifully sculpted grounds were given to the
city as late as 1966 by Mrs Anne Maxwell Macdonald and
now form ★★ **Pollok Country Park** ❻, where morning joggers and evening strollers enjoy the Highland cattle, heavy horses, art collections and woodland walks. The
driveway runs past the police Dog and Mounted Branch
and parkland grazed by 'toffee-wrapper' cattle with their
glowering fringes to ★★★ **Pollok House** ❻ (daily
10am–5pm), a masterful William Adam construction of

Pollok House

Burrell Collection exhibits

Rodin's Thinker

1752. Its exquisite interior retains many original features and houses a fine collection of Spanish School paintings, and the gardens – including a particularly fine parterre and a full and productive walled garden – are bounded by a lazy curve of White Cart Water. It has undergone a sympathetic restoration programme, and there is a good café-bar in the kitchen.

Retracing the route and forking left leads to the internationally famous ★★★ **Burrell Collection** 🌑 (Monday to Thursday and Saturday 10am–5pm, Friday and Sunday 11am–5pm), an outstanding legacy of the shipping magnate Sir William Burrell, whose collector's instincts and eye for a bargain were on a par with his occasional rival William Randolph Hearst. He perfected the business method of selling his fleets of ships in a boom period and buying in a slump, and realised his considerable fortune in 1916 when he sold up to concentrate on his first love, art. The collection is eclectic and idiosyncratic, with more than 9,000 objects from Egypt, Greece, the Middle East and South and East Asia, and tapestries and stained glass from medieval Europe. Favourites with Glasgow visitors are the Degas collection, Rodin's *Thinker* (one of 14 casts made from the original) and the Warwick Vase, an 8-ton marble which dominates the courtyard.

Glasgow city received this fascinating collection in 1944 in a bequest of restrictive conditions, largely concerning Burrell's fears about the potential damage to his treasures from industrial air pollution. This meant that they lay in storage until 1983 when cleaner air and the acquisition of Pollok Estate allowed the construction of an award-winning building whose deceptively simple lines have drawn as much admiration as the contents. Medieval archways from the collection are blended with new red sandstone, and some halls have glass walls to the floor, giving the impression that the exhibits are being viewed in the open air. Others are completely enclosed and provide a warmly lit backdrop for some of the world's most exquisite tapestries. The collection also includes exhibits of entire rooms from Burrell's home at Hutton Castle in Berwickshire and an excellent restaurant and café.

Pollok Park delights in detail

The road out of the park on the left – look out for the carved woodpecker – leads onto Haggs Road. Turn right, get in the middle lane and follow it to Pollokshaws Road and the Round Toll roundabout, then take the B769 for Thornliebank. Stay on this road until the next roundabout and turn left onto the A727 for East Kilbride. Soon after joining the dual carriageway, turn right into Rouken Glen Park.

★ **Rouken Glen** 🌑 was donated to the city by Mr A. Cameron Corbett (later Lord Rowallan) in 1906 and passed to the adjoining Eastwood Council in 1984 after a dispute over running costs. Its loss to Glasgow was felt on an emotional level by many who remembered school trips to the large boating pond, where a motor launch would carry trippers round the islands, much to the indignation of nesting ducks.

Fears of the park's demise, however, were groundless, and a thriving range of commercial concerns – an attractive garden centre, art gallery, Chinese restaurant and a signposted walkabout trail – have given it a new lease of life. The old attractions however, remain unchanged: the waterfall tumbling into a mossy glen, the walled garden, a golf course and generous parkland.

Turning right at the exit, follow the A727 over Eastwood Toll roundabout, through the suburbs of Clarkston to Clarkston Toll, where Greenbank Garden is signposted on the first right after the roundabout.

★★ **Greenbank Garden 70** (garden daily 9.30am–sunset; shop and tearoom, 1 November to 31 March, Saturday and Sunday 2–4pm, 1 April to 31 October, daily 11am–5pm; house, 1 April to 31 October, Sunday 2–4pm), which lies on Flenders Road, off Mearns Road, is a substantial walled garden which many city dwellers regard as an oasis of calm. It is one of the few substantial properties the National Trust for Scotland has close to the city. The gardens surround a tobacco merchant's 18th-century mansion, and tours of the interior with its remarkable billiard room are conducted most Sunday afternoons. A tennis court has been converted into a garden for disabled visitors, with raised beds, and the floral profusion of its parterre layout encourages wildlife.

The quickest way to return to the city is go to Clarkston Toll and follow the signs for the M77, taking junction 3 for the city centre.

Playground in Rouken Glen Park

Statuary in Greenbank Garden

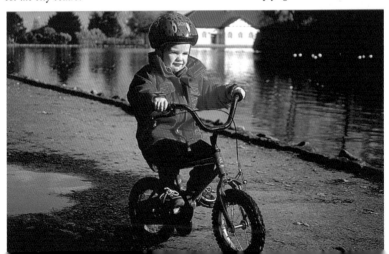

Enjoying Rouken Glen

Route 9

The Mackintosh Tour

House for an Art Lover – Scotland Street School Museum – The Lighthouse – The Willow Tea Rooms – Glasgow School of Art – The Mackintosh House – Queen's Cross Church – The Hill House

The Martyrs' School

House for an Art Lover

Scotland Street School Museum

Rarely has a whole industry been founded on the designs of one architect, but Charles Rennie Mackintosh (1868–1928) was no ordinary architect. His vision and originality were at the forefront of the Modern Movement, and his imaginative buildings and clean, simple interior design were quite unique. One of 13 children of a police superintendent, he was born in Parsons Street, where he would later create the Martyrs' School. He attended night classes in Glasgow's School of Art – then in the McLellan Galleries – before joining Honeyman & Keppie, for whom he did his best work. His first major public building, the former *Glasgow Herald* office – renamed The Lighthouse in a design by Barcelona Olympics maestro Javier Mariscal – was the focal point of Glasgow's year as City of Architecture in 1999. Many of Mackintosh's buildings were neglected until the 1980s, when his importance was realised and restoration commenced. They lie across the city and a comprehensive day tour is difficult, but the following guide highlights the most accessible and representative works, marked with an **Ⓜ** on the maps.

★ **House for an Art Lover** (*see map, page 44*; 1 April to 30 September, Monday to Wednesday 10am–4pm, Thursday to Sunday 10am–1pm; 1 October to 31 March, Saturday and Sunday 10am–1pm; tel: 0141 353 4770) was created from a portfolio which Mackintosh presented for a design competition in 1901. Following his drawings, the house was built in a beautiful parkland setting beside the Victorian walled garden in Bellahouston Park, and contains striking details and interiors as well as a café and shop. The nearest Underground station is Ibrox; mainline station, Dumbreck. The house is about 15 minutes by taxi from the city centre.

★ **Scotland Street School** (*see map, page 44*; Monday to Thursday and Saturday 10am–5pm, Friday and Sunday 11am–5pm) is most easily reached by Underground at Shields Road station, from whose entrance the twin towers of leaded glass and red sandstone stand out from across the road. Built between 1903 and 1906, the school is clearly Glasgow-style.

In the city centre ★★ **The Lighthouse** (*see map, pages 14–15*; Monday, Wednesday to Saturday 10.30am–5pm, Tuesday 11am–5pm, Sunday noon–5pm; www.thelighthouse.co.uk) has a Mackintosh Interpretation Centre to place the artist in his cultural context and to help visitors find his buildings. Built to a Mariscal design beside the tower of the old *Glasgow Herald* building in Mitchell Street, its rooftop platform offers close-up views of his work. It also hosts a variety of temporary exhibitions.

In Buchanan Street is a faithful recreation of the ★ **The Willow Tea Rooms** (*see map, pages 14–15*; Monday to Saturday 9am–5pm, Sunday 11am–5pm, closed Sunday in winter), displaying the innovative design work Mackitosh carried out for well-known restaurateur Kate Cranston at the turn of the century. The originals of the White Room and the Blue Room are in the care of Glasgow City Council.

The Willow Tea Rooms

Along Sauchiehall Street and up Scott Street on the right is Mackintosh's crowning achievement, the ★★ **Glasgow School of Art** (*see map, pages 14–15*; guided tours April to September daily 10am–4pm on the hour; October to March Monday–Saturday 11am and 2pm; www.gsa. ac.uk). One of the most venerable art schools in the UK, every stone, window and railing is redolent of the architect's unique style. The east wing was started in 1897 under the influence of revered headmaster Fra Newbery, but the west wing was not completed until 1909.

Glasgow School of Art

49

In 1906, Mackintosh completely redesigned the interior of an ordinary terrace house at 78 Southpark Avenue for himself and his wife Margaret, whom he had married in 1900 just before being made a full partner in Honeyman & Keppie. They lived in it for eight years and, before it was demolished in 1963, the fittings were removed and are now on display as the ★ **Mackintosh House** (*see map, page 38*) in the **Hunterian Gallery** (*see page 42*; Monday to Saturday 9.30am–5pm), which is a brief taxi ride from the School of Art.

Mackintosh House in the Hunterian Gallery

Another short taxi hop away from here is the ★ **Queen's Cross Church** (*see map, page 38*) in Garscube Road, which is now the headquarters of the **Charles Rennie Mackintosh Society** and is open to visitors. ★★ **The Hill House** (1 April to 31 October, 1.30pm–5.30pm; tel: 01436 673900) is not in Glasgow, but it should be included in any tour of Mackintosh works. A 40-minute train ride away in Helensburgh (First Scotrail, 08457 484950), it is by far the most attractive of his domestic commissions. Built on a commanding site for the publisher Walter Blackie, the fittings have been meticulously conserved by the National Trust for Scotland.

For access arrangements to Mackintosh properties contact the **Charles Rennie Mackintosh Society**, tel: 0141 946 6600; www.crmsociety.com, or contact the **Glasgow Tourist Office**, (*see page 75*). It's worthwhile buying a one-day Mackintosh Trail Ticket (£12) which allows visitors entry to all participating Mackintosh attractions.

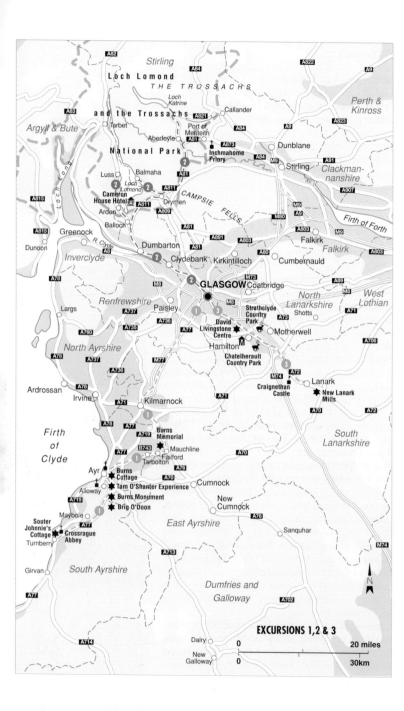

Excursion 1

Burns Country

Mauchline – Highland Mary Monument – Bachelors' Club – Ayr – Burns Cottage – Auld Alloway Kirk – Brig O'Doon – Burns National Heritage Park – Souter Johnnie's Cottage *See map opposite*

For a' that, an' a' that,
It's coming yet for a' that,
That Man to Man, the world o'er,
Shall brothers be for a' that

Scots, with their long tradition of struggle for social justice, are particularly susceptible to the egalitarian theme that runs through the works of the Ploughman Poet, their National Bard, Robert Burns (1759–96). The memory of his turbulent life – a life replete with love, laughter, triumph and despair – is kept alive at Burns Suppers across the world at the end of January, and the minutiae of his dalliances, though a source of fascination for Scots, are fully chronicled elsewhere.

Burns's associations with Glasgow were tenuous – some minor dealings with publishers – but the literary legacy he left and the memorials to his origins in the Burns Country are easily accessible from the city and make a fascinating day out. A car is required for this excursion that takes you down to the southwest coast.

Leave the city on the M8 westbound and join the M77 then the A77 heading for Ayr. Turn off just past Kilmarnock at the A76 signposted for Dumfries. This road leads through typical Ayrshire countryside – rich farmland with copses of wind-beaten trees and straggling streams – to the village of Mauchline, on the outskirts of which stands the red sandstone Scots baronial folly of the **National Burns Memorial Tower**, established in 1896, and worth a look. The **Burns House** (tel: 01290 550045; early May to late September, Tuesday to Sunday 10am–5pm; Easter to October, Tuesday to Sunday 10am–5pm) in which the poet lived is in the village centre, as is **Poosie Nansie's Tavern**, where he was known to take his pleasure. This ale house is said to have inspired part of his cantata *The Jolly Beggars*.

Leaving the village on the B743, the road winds towards ★ **Failford**, a scatter of houses in a small dip. A grassy path behind a sign to Failford Gorge – particularly easy to miss – leads to a monument to **Highland Mary**, the mysterious but beautiful woman for whom Burns wrote *My Highland Lassie O* and from whom he took his last farewell here

National Burns Memorial Tower

Poosie Nansie's Tavern

The Bachelors' Club

Burns Tavern in Ayr

52

The Burns Cottage in Alloway

in 1786. This is one of the lesser Burns monuments, but the simplicity of it is in stark contrast to the Heritage Park at Alloway, and the inscription on the pillar is touching:

That sacred hour can I forget,
Can I forget the hallowed grove,
Where by the winding Ayr we met,
To live one day of parting love.

Past Failford, a brief diversion on the right leads to Tarbolton, a farming community where the National Trust for Scotland is the custodian of the ★ **Bachelors' Club** (tel: 01292 541940; 1 April to 30 September, Friday to Tuesday 1–5pm, last admission 4.30pm; morning visits available for pre-booked groups). It is a 17th-century thatched house just off the main road through the village, where the poet and his cronies formed a debating club with, it has to be said, easy access to the inn next door. It was almost certainly here that Burns was introduced to the Freemasonry which shaped his philosophy of the brotherhood of Man.

Returning to the B743, it is 6 miles (10 km) to ★★ **Ayr**, a bustling resort town with beautiful sandy beaches, excellent shops and a classical statue of Burns in the main square. Crossing the main road over the River Ayr, the 15th-century pedestrian bridge on the left is the **Auld Brig**, the harbour is on the right and the imposing 126ft (38m) pillared steeple straight ahead is Ayr Town Hall. Burns was baptised in the **Auld Kirk**.

Heading out of town on the A719 signposted for Maidens, look for a sign for the Heads of Ayr, then turn left at the first sign for **Alloway**, a pretty village of rose-entwined cottages which is at the heart of the Burns Country. A handy car park on the left at the junction with the B7024 to Maybole serves the ★★ **Burns Cottage** (April to September, daily 10am–5.30pm; October to March, daily 10am–5pm), the birthplace of Burns. It's a clay-wall-and-thatch house, which the poet's father William built with his own hands and where he instilled young Robert's love of language and learning. An original copy of the *Kilmarnock Edition*, the first collection of poems which he published to raise cash in order to emigrate to Jamaica, is held with other mementos in the adjacent **museum.**

It is a short walk from here to the ★★ **Tam O'Shanter Experience**, a visitor centre named after his most famous poem, a tale of warlocks and witches which warns of the dangers of one dram too many. The centre (April to September, 10am–5.30pm; October to March, 10am–5pm) has two audio-visual theatres, bringing the poet and his best-loved tale to life. Visitors are occasionally greeted by a cheerful young man in frock and coat and knee breeches pretending to be the poet.

★★ Auld Alloway Kirk, just a little further on, is a 16th-century refuge which was a ruin even in Burns's day and was last used in 1756. Its gloomy graveyard holds the remains of Burns's father, and the mossy crypts and worn stones with their goblin carvings are a suitably chilling setting for the dance of the witches as the Devil – '*a tousie tyke, black, grim and large*' – played the pipes and '*gart them skirl*'. Those of a nervous disposition should ensure their visit ends before nightfall.

Auld Alloway Kirk

When Tam, inspired by John Barleycorn, interrupted their dance with the shout: '*Weel done, Cutty Sark*', his mare Meg fled to **★ Brig O'Doon** nearby to escape minus '*her ain grey tail*'. The 13th-century cobbled bridge with its ancient arch now stands below the **★ Burns Monument**, a Grecian tower designed by Thomas Hamilton and opened in 1823 at a cost of £2,085. It is surrounded by a garden of heathers and rose bowers which leads to the car park of the **Burns National Heritage Park** (tel: 01292 443700; www.burnsheritagepark.com).

The B7024 carries on to **Maybole**, where Burns's father and mother met in 1756. Joining the A77, signposted for Stranraer, the road leads past the dramatic 13th-century ruins of **Crossraguel Abbey** with its abbot's tower and dovecote, to the village of Kirkoswald. Here the National Trust for Scotland maintains the thatched **★ Souter Johnnie's Cottage** (tel: 01655 760603; 1 April to 30 September, Friday to Tuesday, 11.30am–5pm), a representation of the daily life of the cobbler who was the inspiration behind Tam O'Shanter's '*ancient, trusty, drouthy crony*'.

Souter Johnnie's Cottage

This is a long but fascinating run which could be well rounded off with refreshment in the excellent **Westin Turnberry Resort Hotel** (tel: 01655 331000), just a few miles further south, and scene of memorable moments in Open golf history.

Brig O'Doon

Lake of Menteith

Excursion 2

Loch Lomond and the Trossachs

Balloch – Drymen – Balmaha – Lake of Menteith – Trossachs – Loch Katrine *See map, page 50*

You tak' the High Road,
and I'll tak' the Low Road,
and I'll be in Scotland afore ye.

Loch Lomond: the jetty at Luss

Some features of Luss

The words of the Loch Lomond song distil the romance of the glens for Scots the world over, but for the most part, the reality of the High Road these days is a wide dual carriageway. Following signs for Crianlarich, the A82 continues westwards from Great Western Road in the centre of Glasgow through the western suburbs along the north bank of the Clyde past Bowling, Dumbarton – the ancient capital of Strathclyde, with its castle on the rock – and Balloch.

This is a long excursion, but once at the loch, the roads mellow out and the countryside ranges from the lush and rolling to true Highland drama. The route includes points at which you have to double back on yourself, but generally not for more than a few miles.

The first is at Loch Lomond itself. Still following the Crianlarich signs, head first for the village of ★ **Luss**. Although surrounded on the outskirts by tourist services, the rose-clad cottages and the old pier are still attractive. On the other side of the main carriageway, a farm road signposted for Glen Luss runs up to some of the best hill-walking within easy reach of the city. A series of Corbetts (Scottish hills between 2,500ft/76m) and the 3,000ft/914m Munros afford spectaular views to the Clyde estuary and the western islands. The weather in the mountains can change fairly quickly, so always carry a map, and dress warmly.

Returning south, 7 miles (11km) on, a slip road on the left leads to ★ **Duck Bay Marina** (tel: 01389 751234, a busy hotel, restaurant and bar (10am–midnight) with picnic areas along the shore road. This area, with its easy access to the wide expanse of the southern loch, is popular with jet-skiers and sailors. On the same road is the AA five-star ★ **Cameron House Hotel** (tel: 01389 755565; lounge bar 10am–midnight, various restaurants), a beautiful and luxurious lochside former stately home with first-class spa and golf facilities. You can even arrive by seaplane.

Continuing south, turn left at the roundabout signed for ★ **Balloch** and left again at the next roundabout. This leads into the heart of Loch Lomond's only town of any size. It now hosts Loch Lomond Shores (tel: 01389 722406; www.lomondshores.com), a modern visitor centre with shops, café and innovative aquarium (tel: 01389 721500) complete with sharks, which is the centrepiece of the newly created National Park, Scotland's first. Boats of all shapes and sizes crowd the banks and pontoons as the loch empties into the River Leven on its way to the Clyde.

Balloch

The A811, signposted for Drymen, wanders through undulating farmland, passing only one village of note, Gartocharn, with its atmospheric pub, **The Hungry Monk** (tel: 01389 830448; daily, 11am–midnight). The small hill at the back is called ★ **Duncryne** and is worth the gentle effort of the climb for views across the water-meadows of the southern loch, the wooded islands and the ever higher hills in the distance, including Ben Lomond.

Watering hole in Drymen

At the junction with the A809 turn left to **Drymen**, a delightful village, lying 11 miles (18km) north of Glasgow. It retains a charming rural atmosphere, with the main road winding past the Church of Scotland cemetery and the ★ **Buchanan Arms Hotel** (tel: 01360 660588) to a village square. The cosy **Clachan Inn** (tel: 01360 660824), established in 1734, and on the corner of the square, is a good place to eat, or enjoy a dram.

The B837 from the centre runs 5 picturesque miles (7km) to ★★ **Balmaha**, a village lying on the Highland Boundary Fault, a geological line separating the Highlands from the Lowlands. A scatter of whitewashed houses surround the small inlet where **Balmaha's boatyard** (tel: 01360 870214) caters for fishermen and loch cruisers, and offers places on the regular mailboat round the islands – an unusual day trip. The **West Highland Way**, a 95-mile (152km) walk from Milngavie, on the outskirts of Glasgow, to Fort William, passes through the village. The pleasant **Oak Tree Inn** (tel: 01360 870357) is a good accommodation option or to enjoy hearty pub food and real ale. A path leads from the main

Picturesque Balmaha

Inchmahome Priory

Route planning at the Lodge

*SS Sir Walter Scott
on Loch Katrine*

car park to the Conic Hill, the dramatic rise behind the village from which it is possible to see that the 37 islands in the loch are part of the same geological formation.

Returning to Drymen, the A811 meanders north and east before joining the A81 north across the flatlands towards the hills of the Queen Elizabeth Forest. At the Rob Roy Motel, the route goes left to Aberfoyle, but turning right along the A81 for a short distance to the B8034, brings you to the island priory of ★ **Inchmahome** (April to September, daily 9.30am–4.30am; £4.50 including ferry) on the Lake of Menteith, the only 'lake' in Scotland. These beautiful 12th-century Augustinian remains once sheltered Mary Queen of Scots. The **Lake of Menteith Hotel** (tel: 01877 385258) combines fine cuisine with memorable views over the lake.

On the return to Aberfoyle, follow the A821 for the Trossachs. ★ **Aberfoyle** is a market village and tourist honey-pot, with a variety of pubs and restaurants. The road north negotiates a startling series of hairpin bends as it climbs past the ★ **David Marshall Lodge** to the Duke's Pass – watch out for a kilted piper here in the summer – then descends to Loch Achray. One of the small peaks on the far side of the loch is ★ **Ben A'an** and, like Duncryne, more than richly rewards the effort of conquering it. It affords an unparalleled vista of Loch Katrine, which has changed only in minor detail since Sir Walter Scott was inspired by the scenery to write *The Lady of The Lake* (1810). Before Ben A'an, the main road branches off to ★ **Loch Katrine**, where the steam yacht *Sir Walter Scott* sails on Glasgow's water supply (April to October; for times, tel: 01877 376316). Bicycles are also available to hire for a recommended ride along the lovely lochside road.

For the quickest journey back to Glasgow, travel the 10 miles (16km) to Callander, then on to Stirling to join the M9.

Excursion 3

The Clyde Valley

Strathclyde Country Park – Duke of Hamilton's Mausoleum – David Livingstone Centre – Chatelherault Country Park – Craignethan Castle – Lanark – New Lanark *See map, page 50*

The River Clyde, the wonderful Clyde,
The name of it thrills me and fills me with pride

When Glaswegians sing maudlin praise of the river that gave their city meaning, they think of the clatter of shipyards and the sway of giant cranes. But further down the valley is an altogether different river, wandering through gentle hills and watering fertile orchards and fruit farms. This tour requires a car, or a bike for the very fit.

The M8 snakes through the centre of Glasgow, and it is possible to join it at many points. Once on the eastbound carriageway, follow signs for Carlisle and Edinburgh through the industrial eastern suburbs until Junction 8 with the M73, then follow signs for Carlisle.

The first stop should be **Hamilton**, a busy town off the A723. On the left is ★ **Strathclyde Country Park**, accessible via junction 5 of the M74, a huge recreation area with a man-made loch that offers sailing, windsurfing and water-skiing, and also a permanent amusement park with some of the biggest rides in Scotland. On the right is the town itself, which has long association with the Covenanters, religious freedom fighters who fought protracted and bloody campaigns for their beliefs and gave rise to the Cameronians, a locally raised regiment whose battle honours are gathered from around the world.

Strathclyde Country Park

The **Low Parks Museum** (Monday to Saturday 10am–5pm, Sunday noon–5pm), built on the site of the Hamilton Palace, complete with new mezzanine café, is located on Muir Street. It tells the turbulent history of the town, its regiment and the Hamilton family, whose spectacular ★ **Mausoleum**, built by the 10th Duke in the 1840s, has impassive stone lions guarding the enormous bronze doors and beautiful marblework within.

Guarding the Mausoleum

A few miles up the A724 at Blantyre is the ★ **David Livingstone Centre** (April to December, Monday to Saturday 10am–5pm, Sunday 12.30pm–5pm), a memorial to Scotland's greatest missionary explorer, who was born here in 1813. Growing up as a poor factory boy, he led an eventful life which included the discovery of the Victoria Falls on the border between Zambia and Zimbabwe while on a journey across the African

David Livingstone Centre

Chatelherault Country Park

continent in 1855. He died of disease in 1873 while searching for the then unknown source of the Nile.

Returning through Hamilton, join the A72 for Lanark and, as the suburbs give way to countryside, the gates of ★★ **Chatelherault Country Park** (April to September, Monday to Saturday 10am–5pm, Sunday noon–5.30pm; October to March, Monday to Saturday 10am–5pm, Sunday noon–5pm) open up on the right. A Visitor Centre, once the kennels for the hunting dogs of the Duke of Hamilton, butts onto the main building, designed by William Adam for the 5th Duke and completed in 1744. The building fell into dereliction – mining subsidence has added a jaunty slope to some floors – and a masterful restoration was completed in 1987 allowing full appreciation of the superb plasterwork showing ornate figures from classical mythology. At the same time, development of nearly 500 acres (200 hectares) of the Avon Gorge, one of the least polluted of the Clyde's tributaries, created the park with miles of riverside walks, the dramatic Duke's Bridge, the medieval mystery of Cadzow Castle, and rolling parkland featuring cattle whose lineage dates back to Roman times and whose temper should not be tried.

The A72 now follows the twists and turns of the Clyde as it runs through a valley of soft-fruit, tomato and vegetable growers, past Dalserf's 1655 church and the pretty half-timbered village of Rosebank with its three-star Popinjay Hotel (tel: 01555 860441). Slightly further on, a sign points right to ★ **Craignethan Castle** (April to September, Monday to Sunday 9.30am–6.30pm; 1 November to 31 March, Saturday 9.30pm–5.30pm, Sunday 2–4.30pm, last entry 4pm), a sombre keep situated 2 miles (3km) up a narrow and twisting road. Dating back to around 1530, this rambling ruin was one of the last great family tower fortresses, and from it the Hamilton family played a pivotal role in Scottish politics, including their support for Mary Queen of Scots, whom they sheltered here after her abdication in 1567.

Craignethan Castle

Although Sir Walter Scott denied that its ivy-clad ruins were the inspiration for Tillietudlem Castle in the Waverley novel *Old Mortality* – and indeed he is said to have considered settling here instead of Abbotsford – its remote location and air of mystery are resonant for many of Claverhouse and the Covenanting bands.

Back on the A72, the road continues through Kirkfieldbank to the historic town of ★ **Lanark**, a slope trodden during the Wars of Independence (1286–1328) by the raggle-taggle hordes of William Wallace, whose statue looks down from an 18th-century church along a bustling main street divided by pretty floral displays. This busy market town was founded in 1140 by King David, who established a castle here, which has long since disappeared.

Following the signs at the top of the street for New Lanark, the road twists down again to the Clyde and one of the most remarkable episodes in Scotland's industrial history and one of its most adventurous heritage restoration projects. At first sight, ★★★ **New Lanark** (tel: 01555 661345; June to August daily 10.30am–5pm; September to May 11am–5pm) seems little more than a group of stone-built warehouses, but it was here that David Dale and his son-in-law Robert Owen conducted a social experiment that was to have lasting repercussions for the bitterly oppressed working classes.

Dale, from Stewarton, made his fortune in weaving and French yarns and in 1785, using the abundant water power of the Clyde, set up the New Lanark Mills which, at their height, employed over 2,000 workers, many of them children. Along with Owen, who assumed management in 1799, he introduced a regime of decent housing, reasonable wages, education and health care, to prove his theory that contented workers were productive workers. His message did as much to create a social revolution as the mills had done for industry, and as a result workers' rights began to be considered seriously elsewhere.

New Lanark: decent housing for the workers

The village, now a UNESCO World Heritage site, has been restored as a living community complete with hotel and shops, and the millworkers' tenement rows are desirable properties. There is also a youth hostel here (tel: 0870 004 1143). In the Visitor Centre, a chair ride called the Millennium Experience compares in audio-visuals the life in the mill, past, present, and future.

Along the river, a sylvan walk leads to the Falls of Clyde, where the Scottish Wildlife Trust organise badger watches, and the keen-eyed may spot kingfishers, owls and pipistrelle bats as night descends.

A model of restoration

Architecture

Opposite: Glasgow School of Art

Glasgow has been called the easternmost city of the United States, and, although its citizens may like to think of themselves in the same manner as New Yorkers, the solid confidence of its Victorian architecture and the cohesive grid plan of its city centre is more reminiscent of Chicago.

For many years its reputation was as blighted as the lives of its people by slums and dreadful degradation. But it should be remembered that the slums invariably started out as attempts to alleviate existing and often worse social conditions, just as the currently maligned peripheral housing estates and high-rises were welcomed as beneficent release from the cramped city-centre tenements. And, although Glasgow has a feast of classical architecture to offer, one of the deciding factors in the City of Architecture award was the emphasis on community living.

In the city centre, however, extravagance and drama in sculpted stone predominates. From the weathered 13th-century remnants around Glasgow Cathedral *(see Route 1)* and the 17th-century mercantile optimism around the Trongate, to the grandeur of the mansions of the Tobacco Lords in the Merchant City in the 18th century *(see Route 3)* and the robust flowering of the Victorians, Glasgow developed into a city carved painstakingly from sandstone.

61

Although Charles Rennie Mackintosh *(see Route 9)* and Alexander 'Greek' Thomson are foremost in the current view of Glasgow's architectural heritage, others such as William Young – who created the City Chambers *(see Route 4)* as a monument to civic pride in 1888 – J.T. Rochead, J.J. Burnet and Charles Wilson contributed mightily. Rochead's work in St Vincent Street sets the tone for the commercial centre, and his Grosvenor Hotel is a Venetian marvel; Burnet's former TSB banking hall on the corner of Ingram Street and Glassford Street outshines the bigger surroundings; Wilson created an Italianate skyscape in the Park Circus area *(see Route 6)* unequalled in Britain.

Huge enterprises like Robert Anderson's Central Hotel and the Edwardian mass of the Royal Technical College (now the University of Strathclyde) vie for attention with small-scale confections like James Miller's miniature version of Azay-le-Rideau in the centre of St Enoch Square.

Modern architecture in Glasgow is following a bold tradition. Atlantic Quay on the Clyde has fitting waterfront grandeur, as does the the new Clyde Auditorium by Sir Norman Foster and the Glasgow Science Centre complex, with its dramatic viewing tower. The interior of the new BBC Scotland building on Pacific Quay is equally bold; so, too, is the Clyde Arc Bridge. Italian Centre and Princes Square are splendid examples of how to rescue dilapidated warehouses and transform them into shopping meccas to envy.

Design to the last detail

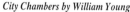

City Chambers by William Young

Foster's Clyde Auditorium

Tranquillity in Kelvingrove Park

Queen's Park

Parks

The Victorians viewed public parks as the lungs of their smoky cities, allowing their workers the physically and morally beneficial effects of clean air and uplifting scenery. **Glasgow Green** was the only public space in the city until 1846, when a grand plan was proposed by the council to create three huge sculpted parklands – **Kelvingrove** *(see Route 6)* in the west, **Alexandra Park** in the east and **Queen's Park** *(see Route 8)* in the south – under the hand of designer Sir Joseph Paxton, of Crystal Palace fame.

The city now has more than 70 parks, and, although the recreations reflect Victorian tastes – boating ponds, playgrounds, putting, bowling – the work of the inventive and industrious Parks Department has given each its own character. The following are also worth a visit:

Victoria Park, Scotstoun – beautiful formal gardens and raised decorative beds, substantial boating pond, and the site of the Fossil Grove, a covered excavation of tree stumps in a forest area dating back 330 million years.

Linn Park, off Clarkston Road – lovely walks along the banks of White Cart Water, and the ruins of a 14th-century castle on Court Knowe, from where Mary Queen of Scots is said to have looked across at the Battle of Langside.

Botanic Gardens, Great Western Road *(see Route 7)* – extensive grounds on the banks of the River Kelvin which contain the spectacular circular glasshouse of the Kibble Palace.

Bellahouston Park, Dumbreck Road – the site of the visit to Glasgow by Pope John Paul II in 1982, Bellahouston has splendid views over the city from its central hill. Attractions include a dry ski slope and the House for an Art Lover *(see Route 9)*.

Performing Arts

Since a municipal decision was taken to consider the city as a cultural rather than industrial centre, the arts and the accompanying nightlife have blossomed. While Glasgow may not yet have an event to compare with the Edinburgh International Festival, Scottish national organisations provide a cultural spread to satisfy the most eclectic tastes. For details of performance times and dates, see the local press, or visit www.seeglasgow.com.

Scottish Opera performance of Mozart's Magic Flute

Scottish Opera is regarded as the jewel in the crown. In its refurbished Victorian **Theatre Royal** home (tel: 0870 060 6647) on Hope Street, the company consistently coaxes world-class performances from international guests, a stable of domestic singers and a renowned chorus. Founded by Sir Alexander Gibson in 1975, in previous incarnations the Theatre Royal's boards have been trodden by Sarah Bernhardt, Harry Lauder and Ellen Terry. This majestic venue also provides the perfect setting for major productions by **Scottish Ballet** (tel: 0141 331 2931). Nearby, on McPhate Street in Cowcaddens, those who enjoy the skirl of the bagpipes will love **The National Piping Centre** and its museum (tel: 0141 353 0220).

The **Glasgow Royal Concert Hall** (tel: 0141 353 8000), at the north end of Buchanan Street, was completed just in time for the City of Culture celebrations in 1990. Its splendid acoustics attract orchestras of international reputation, and it hosts regular performances by the **Royal Scottish National Orchestra**, (tel: 0141 226 3868; www.rsno.org.uk) currently under the baton of Stéphane Denève. The Green Room, its restaurant, is a refined dining experience. Half a mile east of here lie the refurbished City Halls and the Old Fruitmarket in the Merchant City area, home of the **BBC Scottish Symphony Orchestra** and the Scottish Music Centre (tel: 0141 353 8000).

The Citizens Theatre

The **Citizens Theatre** (tel: 0141 429 0022) in Gorbals Street, also has international standing. It surprised the arts world over many years by offering from its Gorbals home cutting-edge, iconoclastic drama coupled with theatre design of stunning originality. Also on the South Side is the **Tramway** (tel: 0141 422 2023), a huge and exciting theatre space converted from a depot for the tramcars which were once Glasgow's most commonly used public transport. By late 2008, Scottish Ballet will relocate here.

The National Lottery financed part of the redevelopment of the **Tron Theatre** (tel: 0141 552 4267; www.tron.co.uk) in the centre of town at the Trongate. It not only specialises in recent, often hard-hitting Scottish drama, busy music nights and comedy, but also produces deliciously home-spun pantomime every Christmas. More traditional fare, including large-scale musicals and

The King's Theatre

Checking out the Pavilion

household-name comedians such as Billy Connolly, appear at **The King's Theatre** (tel: 0141 240 1111) in Bath Street, with Glasgow-based shows at the **Pavilion** in Renfield Street (tel: 0870 060 6648).

The **Scottish Exhibition and Conference Centre** (tel: 0141 248 3000) stands on reclaimed dockland on the Clyde's north bank and assumes most of the functions of the old Kelvin Hall. Although its industrial exterior and its acoustics as a concert hall have been criticised, the centre has been a successful venture, billboarding stars as diverse as Bob Dylan and Coldplay, and also bringing in major international conference business. The adjacent **Clyde Centre** – dubbed the Armadillo – hosts smaller concerts.

Henry Wood Hall (tel: 0141 225 3555), at 73 Claremont Street, is a beautiful venue in a former church, mainly used for classical events.

Festivals

For further up-to-date details of forthcoming events and festivals throughout the year, visit: www.glasgow.gov.uk. In the dark days of **January**, a celebration of Celtic musical culture from Brittany to Barra to Cape Breton is held at venues throughout the city for the festival of **Celtic Connections**, which is centred around the Glasgow Royal Concert Hall. The Concert Hall is also the venue for the **RSNO Proms** throughout **June**, which give Scotland's premier orchestra the chance to show its versatility with a range of classical favourites. The **West End Festival**, a concoction of community events, carnival and concerts concentrated in the student area around Byres Road and Kelvingrove Park is also in **June** for three weeks.

Jazz Festival performance

The **Glasgow Jazz Festival** attracts top names like Nina Simone and Buddy Guy and local talent such as Tommy Smith and Bobby Wishart to a colourful venue in the Old Fruitmarket in Albion Street in mid-to late **June** (www.jazz fest.co.uk). The cobbled streets and colonial-style balconies of the market, which lay derelict and hidden for many years, are reminiscent of Bourbon Street in New Orleans.

Summer in the City

Summer in the City fills George Square for two weeks at the start of **July** with a programme of high-profile bands, sports activities, children's events and street theatre. Recent additions to the festival scene in the city include an **International Comedy Festival** in March/April and the **Merchant City Festival** in September. During the last two weeks of **July**, the 800-year-old **Glasgow Fair** is celebrated on Glasgow Green in time-honoured fashion. Though the smash-hit **T in the Park** music festival now hosts thousands of music fans and top-drawer bands in the fields of Perthshire, the somewhat more intimate interior of King Tut's Wah Wah Hut on St Vincents Street continues to showcase some of the best emerging talent.

Visual Arts

A Jake Harvey sculpture at the Hunterian

Glasgow is a gallery-going city. A long-term policy of free access has encouraged enthusiastic attendances at many of the grand municipal galleries and has a spin-off effect on the multitude of smaller private enterprises.

The most prestigious is the recently refurbished **Kelvingrove Art Gallery and Museum**, with an enviable collection of paintings from all the major European schools, particularly 17th-century Dutch, Impressionist and post-Impressionist and the Scottish Colourists.

The **Burrell Collection** in Pollok Country Park is the other major venue, with an unparalleled display of ceramics, silver and tapestries, and French 19th-century art with works by Degas, Manet and Cézanne. Nearby is **Pollok House**, where the Maxwells' Spanish collection includes major paintings by El Greco, Murillo and Goya.

The **Hunterian Art Gallery** in Hillhead Street specialises in European art, British portraiture, a reconstruction of the Mackintosh House and the remarkable Whistler collection. In Castle Street, the **St Mungo Museum of Religious Life and Art** is a relative newcomer in the shadow of the Cathedral, with displays featuring art and artefacts of the world's major religions. In Royal Exchange Square, the collection in the **Gallery of Modern Art** can be controversial, but is always a challenging experience. **The Lighthouse** on Mitchell Lane is a dedicated centre for architecture and design with a changing programme of exhibitions. **The Collins Gallery** in Richmond Street is attached to the University of Strathclyde, and hosts visiting exhibitions. Smaller galleries worth a visit include **Glasgow Print Studios** and the **Transmission Gallery**, both in King Street, and the **Compass Gallery** and **Cyril Gerber Fine Art**, both in West Regent Street.

The Lighthouse

St Mungo Museum

Food and Drink

Opposite: Al fresco dining in the city centre

Malmaison waiter

Restaurants, cafés, bars and pubs flourish like spring flowers in Glasgow, individually and colourfully, to meet increasingly cosmopolitan tastes. Restaurateurs like Ken McCulloch and chefs like Gordon Ramsay and Nick Nairn have been in the vanguard of stylish, modern eating and have lifted standards to such an extent that the city can now offer not only a comprehensive range of international cuisines – including Japanese, Russian and Mongolian – but also some exciting environments enhanced by a strong flair for radical design. For a comprehensive list of where to eat, drink and be merry in Glasgow, visit www.glasgowguide.co.uk/food. Another great source of information is the authoritative *Edinburgh and Glasgow Eating and Drinking Guide*.

Restaurant selection

£££ Expensive (over £55 for two); **££** Moderate (£35–55 for two); **£** Inexpensive (under £35 for two); not including drinks.

An Lochan, 340 Crow Road, West End, tel: 0141 338 6606, closed Monday. Run by owners of the respected An Lochan Hotel in Tighnabruaich, this is another restaurant that reminds diners why Scotland is renowned for its seafood. Relaxed ambience. **££**

Arisaig, 140 St Vincent Street, tel: 0141 204 5399. Airy, modern-style eatery that offers modern Scottish cooking with flair. **££**

Balbir's, 7 Church Street, West End, tel: 0141 339 7711. Don't let the soulless interior fool you. This is an excellent choice for a quick curry full of flavour and fresh ingredients. **£–££**

Café Gandolfi, 64 Albion Street, tel: 0141 552 6813. Another long-established favourite, with flowing wooden furniture by Tim Stead and a lovely loft bar. **££**

City Merchant, 97–99 Candleriggs, tel: 0141 553 1577, closed Sunday. Excellent service, with good, modern Scottish cuisine specialising in meat and seafood. **£££**

The Dhabba, 44 Candleriggs, Merchant City, tel: 0141 553 1249. Glasgow has many fine Indian restaurants, and for those seeking great-value, refined Indian cuisine The Dhabba won't disappoint. **££**

Michael Caines at ABode

Gamba, 225a West George Street, tel: 0141 572 0899, closed Sunday. Fresh local seafood, including oysters and lobster and hints of the Mediterranean, form the mainstay of this fabulous restaurant. **££**

Ichiban Japanese Noodle Restaurant, 50 Queen Street, tel: 0141 204 4200. Minimalist, with steaming bowls of noodles served on long benches. **£**

Popular for Chinese

Malmaison promotions

Ubiquitous Chip

Loon Fung, 417 Sauchiehall Street, tel: 0141 332 1477. Long-established but still admirable Cantonese cuisine, much frequented by the Chinese community. ££

Lux, 1051 Great Western Road, tel: 0141 576 7576. Clean, crisp design and artistically presented food to match in this enterprise by proprietor and chef Stephen Johnson. ££

Malmaison Brasserie, 278 West George Street, tel: 0141 572 1003. This establishment, occupying a former church, sources the best from local food producers. A treat. ££

Michael Caines at ABode, 129 Bath Street, tel: 0141 572 6011. Martin Donnelly is in charge of this stylish fine-dining eatery overseen by Michelin-starred chef Michael Caines. A real taste of Scotland – including scallops and Stornoway black pudding. £££

Millennium Hotel Brasserie, George Square, tel: 0141 332 6711. Elegant eating in a splendid city-centre location, with conservatory to watch goings-on in the square. ££

Mussel Inn, 157 Hope Street, tel: 0141 572 1405. Features the best of west-coast seafood – oysters, scallops, prawns and, of course, mussels. ££

Naked Soup, 6 Kersland Street, West End, tel: 0141 334 8999. This trendy, wood-panelled eatery is where to find honest, hearty and delicious lunchtime fare. £

No. Sixteen, 16 Byres Road, tel: 0141 339 2544. No. Sixteen serves impressive food at remarkably down-to-earth prices with an interesting wine list. ££

Rab Ha's, 83 Hutcheson Street, Merchant City, tel: 0141 572 0400. Named after a 19th-century local glutton, this cosy restaurant will see you devouring seafood and meat classics from a simple but mouth-watering menu. ££

The Restaurant at Sloans, 62 Argyle Arcade, 108 Argyle Street, tel: 0141 221 8886. An Edwardian-style restaurant serving modern British cuisine. ££

Rogano, 11 Exchange Place, tel: 0141 248 4055. Glasgow's homage to the days of ocean liners and cocktails, exuding the glamour of a 1930s movie. Expensive, but top-class service. This is the place for oysters. Dress to impress. £££

Schottische, 16–18 Blackfriars Street, Merchant City, tel: 0141 552 5055, closed Sunday–Monday. Lovely, cosy restaurant above the popular Babbity Bowster pub. French-influenced cuisine is hearty, flavoursome and with Scottish leanings such as stovies and black pudding. ££

Stravaigin, 28 Gibson Street, Hillhead, tel: 0141 334 2665. Award-winning restaurant using finest fresh local ingredients. Big menu but satisfying result. ££

Two Fat Ladies, 118a Blythswood Street, tel: 0141 847 0088. This newish addition to Glasgow's dining scene guarantees loads of seafood and enticing desserts. ££

Ubiquitous Chip, 12 Ashton Lane, tel: 0141 334 5007. The Chip is an institution in a converted mews stable. Fresh Scottish ingredients, wonderful wine list. Terrific. £££

Pubs and bars

Drinking has always been a serious business in Glasgow, but liberal licensing has taken some of the urgency out of it. Some of the best hostelries are:

Babbity Bowster, 16–18 Blackfriars Street (Monday to Saturday 11am–midnight, Sunday 12.30pm–midnight). Heaving bar that attracts an eclectic mix of media types and local worthies. Great pint, good music.

Bargo, 80 Albion Street (all week 11am–midnight). Set in the heart of the Merchant City. Good for lunches, busier at night. Excellent Staropramen lager.

Blackfriars, 36 Bell Street (all week noon–midnight). A big, friendly bar with a range of real ale beers and frequently changing guest beers. Excellent comedy club.

Brel, 37–43 Ashton Lane (Monday to Saturday noon–midnight, Sunday 12.30pm–midnight). Rustic, cast-iron furniture and a taste of Belgian food and beer is the order of the day in this popular former coach house.

Budda, 142 St Vincent Street (Sunday to Thursday 11am–1pm, Friday and Saturday 11am–3pm). A smart, after-office crowd goes to this easygoing, stylish Thai-influenced bar in the city centre. Cocktails and Thai food under one roof.

Corinthian, 191 Ingram Street (daily noon–3am). This huge, rather grand former banking hall now offers a number of eating and drinking options.

Horseshoe Bar, 17 Drury Lane (Monday to Saturday 11am–midnight, Sunday 12.30pm–midnight). Always lively, the Horseshoe has a bar that goes on for ever, so there's no problem getting a good, cheap pint.

Jinty McGinty's, 23 Ashton Lane (Monday to Thursday 11am–11pm, Friday and Saturday 11am–midnight, Sunday, 12.30pm–11pm). A heaving Irish bar with good live music and literary quotations round the walls.

Tennent's, 191 Byres Road (Monday to Thursday 11am–11pm, Friday and Saturday 11am–midnight, Sunday 12.30pm–11pm). A drinking pub with a good social mix and a wide choice of ales in the student quarter.

Uisge Beatha, 232–246 Woodlands Road (Monday to Saturday noon–midnight, Sunday 12.30pm–midnight). Kilted bar staff, old-world ambience and a great pint.

Brel in Ashton Lane

Cafés

If you are looking for a quick coffee or sandwich, you'll find a cluster of coffee shops around Royal Exchange Square, slap bang in the city centre.

Fressh, 51 Cochrane Street (Monday to Friday 8am–4pm, Saturday 9am–5pm, Sunday 11am–5pm). Terrific 'hip' option for a smoothie or freshly made sandwich. It's Glasgow's only juice bar.

Tennent's

The bar at The Arches

The opulent Arta

Strawberry Fields

Clubs

Glasgow's club scene has state-of-the-art technology and upfront visiting DJs. Below is a representative selection:

Archaos, 25 Queen Street, tel: 0141 204 3189. Commercial house club on three levels for a mainstream crowd, including hip-hop and R&B.

The Arches, 253 Argyle Street, tel: 0141 565 1000. For the more serious clubber, with big-name DJs.

Arta, 62 Albion Street, tel: 0141 552 2101. Two clubs compete for attention within the trendy warrens of this Mediterranean-style restaurant, bar and club. Popular classics to easy-orchestra to full-on DJs and live bands.

Bamboo, 51 West Regent Street, tel: 0141 332 1067. A busy haunt offering a mix of R&B, hip-hop and soul.

Barrowland, 244 Gallowgate, tel: 0141 552 4601. This is a classic venue for big rock and pop bands.

The Buff, 142 Bath Lane, tel: 0141 248 1777. Trendy and eclectic DJs dish out the tunes to an enthusiastic young crowd eager to hear 'Burn Junk and Old School at the Buff'.

Cathouse, 15 Union Street, tel: 0141 248 6606. Glasgow's rock and alternative club. Open five nights a week.

Cube, 33 & 44 Queen Street, tel: 0141 226 8990. Open all week. Cheap drink and music to suit popular tastes.

The Garage, 490 Sauchiehall Street, tel: 0141 332 1120. The Garage plays the best of Britpop to a large crowd who like cheap entry and cheaper drink. Students galore.

Polo Lounge, 84 Wilson Street, tel: 0141 553 1221. Gay club for professional people. Upmarket surroundings.

Strawberry Fields, 56 Oswald Street, tel: 08450 539289. Rock venue where live bands play through the week.

The Tunnel, 84 Mitchell Street, tel: 0141 204 1000. Ranks as a superclub, has released its own CD and is online.

Shopping

Glaswegians, rightly or wrongly, pride themselves on having a measure of style, and the retail business in recent years has been keen to cater to it. Generally accepted as Britain's most exciting shopping city outside London, the city has attracted top international names and has set the pace in the development of attractive malls.

Princes Square

But before heading to **Buchanan Galleries**, **Princes Square** and **Buchanan Street** *(see Route 4)*, it is worth a look at some of the more idiosyncratic shopping. Starting at London Road off the High Street, pop into Glickman's Confectionery for a taste of sweeties of yesteryear. At Glasgow Cross and walking along the busy Trongate, turn left into **Chisholm Street**, which houses small outlets offering alternative records, tropical fish and tattoos from Terry Tattoo Artist. It is crossed at the bottom by **Parnie Street**, which offers an eclectic mix of specialist shops including the Art Exposure Gallery, A1 Books & Comics, model shops and collectables stores.

For tattoos in Chisholm Street

Going right, **King Street** has a number of worthwhile galleries, including the Original Print Studio, with artists such as Elizabeth Blackadder, the Street Level Gallery, Transmission and Photoworks. Further down King Street is a circus shop and the King's Court antiques market.

Opposite, along Osborne Street, is the massive greenhouse of the **St Enoch Centre**. The BHS entrance leads through the store into the girdered central atrium and what is effectively an indoor street. Escalators and outside elevators lead to the upper shops, such as Debenhams.

St Enoch Centre

At the St Enoch Square exit, a small Victorian folly now houses the **Travel Centre**. This is the last remnant of a grand Victorian piazza which was fronted by one of the city's great railway hotels, demolished to make way for the shopping centre, and where in times past, Highlanders would carry city ladies in sedan chairs. This opens north onto **Argyle Street**. On the left is the bridge of the Central Station, formerly known as the Highlandman's Umbrella, since so many Gaelic migrants congregated there, and, on the right, a stretch of high-street chains.

Going left and then right, **Union Street** – a mix of major and local stores – continues onto Renfield Street, which runs up the hill to **Sauchiehall Street**, probably Glasgow's best-known thoroughfare. It is pedestrianised as far as Rose Street and is lined with shops, including a Waterstones bookshop, pubs, clubs and restaurants.

Sauchiehall Street continues for nearly 2 miles (3km) to the West End, where **Byres Road** *(see Route 7)* has small specialist shops with a leaning towards original design, which create a cosmopolitan atmosphere fitting for the heart of the student quarter.

Getting There

By air

Glasgow has an excellent international airport to the west at Abbotsinch, tel: 0870 040 0008, which is served by flights from all main UK airports and has connections to Europe and North America. It has direct motorway links to the city centre, a journey of about 15 minutes. A taxi to the city centre costs around £20 from a rank outside the terminal building. Buses (£3.95 one way) run daily every seven to 15 minutes 24 hours a day, to Buchanan Bus Station. Buses run every 30 minutes between 11.30pm and 4.30am. The Paisley Gilmour Street Railway Station is closest to the airport; around eight trains an hour depart for the city centre.

British Airways and British Midland operate shuttle flights from London. British Airways, tel: 0870 850 9850, starts flights from Heathrow at 7am Monday to Sunday with the last flight Monday to Friday at 9.45pm. British Midland, tel: 0870 607 0555, www.flybmi.com, starts flights at 7am throughout the week ending at 11pm. Easyjet, tel: 0870 600 0000, www.easyjet.com, flies from Luton 7.55am to 8.55pm Monday to Friday, 8.40am to 9.40pm Saturday and 11.55am to 9.15pm Sunday. Easyjet also flies to London Stansted. Ryanair, tel: 0870 728 0280, www.ryanair.com, operates from Stansted to Prestwick, which is about 40 minutes from Glasgow but has efficient road and rail links. There are also direct flights available to various other UK, European and North American destinations. For details on flights, and to book tickets online, visit: www.glasgowairport.com.

By car

From the south, the west-coast route follows the M1 to Birmingham, then the M6 to the Scottish border, then the A74 and M74, which joins the M8 into the city. The slower east coast route follows the M1 and A1 into Edinburgh, then the cross-country M8 to Glasgow. From the north, the A9 joins the M9 near Stirling and then the M80, A80 and M8 into Glasgow.

By coach

National Express runs a regular coach service from all points in England and Wales into Buchanan Bus Station, tel: 0870 580 8080, or visit www.nationalexpress.com.

By rail

Virgin Railways, tel: 0845 722 2333, www.virgintrains.co.uk, operates the main west-coast route from London, Birmingham and Manchester; standby fares are cheaper but subject to availability. Queen Street Station has a shuttle to Edinburgh and serves the north. For general rail enquiries in Glasgow and Scotland see www.firstgroup.com/scotrail, tel: 08457 550033. Buy tickets online at www.thetrainline.com.

73

Airport arrivals

The M8 motorway

Getting Around

On foot

A colour-coded sign system facilitates navigation of the city centre and main visitor areas. The distinctive blue panels provide directions and information about sights, maps and pedestrian routes. The Glasgow Tourist Information Centre at George Square sells a Glasgow Tourist map for 50p.

Options along Kelvin Way

By public transport

Glasgow's subway network is one of the oldest in the world, but 15 stations on a 24-minute circular track mean that no journey will take longer than 12 minutes. Packages are available, such as the Family Day Tripper Tickets (unlimited travel on First Scotrail services, subway, some ferries and many bus operators). The Subway's 'Discovery' ticket is good value. For £1.90 you can enjoy one day's unlimited travel after 9.30am Monday to Saturday and all day Sunday. Above ground, First Scotrail (www.firstgroup.com/scotrail) runs the extensive rail network. City Sightseeing Glasgow runs open-air bus tours from George Square.

Car hire

Glasgow city-centre traffic is heavy, but a car is useful for excursions to outlying areas. Here is a selection of car-hire firms in Glasgow: Arnold Clark, tel: 0141 434 0480; Avis, tel: 0870 608 6339; Europcar, tel: 0141 418 0040.

Parking

Car parks are plentiful but busy, with spaces around St Enoch Square filled by mid-morning. Multi-storey car parks are at Mitchell Street, Cambridge Street, Montrose Street, Waterloo Street, Oswald Street and Buchanan Galleries. Unauthorised parking is not advisable, as tow-away trucks and clamping units abound. If your accommodation is in the West End, take the subway into the city centre.

Taxis

Black taxis are licensed by Glasgow City Council and can be flagged down in the street but there are also many private taxi firms which are slightly cheaper.

City cab

Cycling

There are great cycle paths, including the 21-mile (34km) Glasgow to Loch Lomond Cycleway, from Bell's Bridge, beside the Clyde Auditorium on the Clyde, to Balloch. Bikes are carried free on all Strathclyde Passenger Transport-supported rail services. For information on cycle routes, visit www.sustrans.org.uk, tel: 0845 113 0065, or ask for the *Clyde and Loch Lomond Cycleway* leaflet at the tourist office.

GLASGOW SUBWAY
SPT

Hillhead · Kelvinbridge (Park and Ride) · St George's Cross · Cowcaddens

Kelvinhall

Partick (Rail Interchange)

Buchanan Street (Rail Interchange)

St Enoch

River   Clyde

Govan

Bridge Street (Park and Ride)

Ibrox · Cessnock · Kinning Park · Shields Road (Park and Ride) · West Street (Park and Ride)

Facts for the Visitor

The Glasgow Tourist Information Centre, 11 George Square (Monday to Saturday 9am–7pm, May, June and September; 9am–8pm, July to August; 9am–6pm, October to April; Sunday 10am–6pm, all year; tel: 0141 204 4400; www.seeglasgow.com), provides practical guidance to getting around the city and the surrounding areas. Staff are on hand to help with information on tours and the city's historical and cultural attractions as well as accommodation. The tourist office also contains a bureau de change, an accommodation booking service and a small shop.

Tourist Information Centre

Travel services
American Express, 115 Hope Street, tel: 0870 600 1060; Thomas Cook, 15–17 Gordon Street, tel: 0845 308 9309. Also at 50 Sauchiehall Street, tel: 0845 308 9313.

Cash dispensers and link machines
Abbey, 84 Argyle Street; Bank of Scotland, 54–62 Sauchiehall Street; Barclays, 90 St Vincent Street; Clydesdale Bank, 200 Buchanan Street (Buchanan Galleries); Royal Bank of Scotland, 8 Gordon Street; Lloyds TSB, 52–60 St Vincent Street; Woolwich, 18 Gordon Street. RBS has approximately 15 cash machines in the city centre, including at Queen Street Station.

Emergency services
Fire, Police, Ambulance, tel: 999
Strathclyde Police HQ, 173 Pitt Street, tel: 0141 532 2000
Royal Infirmary, Castle Street, tel: 0141 211 4000
Western Infirmary, Dumbarton Road, tel: 0141 211 2000
Fire HQ, north of the river, Port Dundas Road, tel: 0141 302 3333; south of the river, McFarlane Street, tel: 0141 552 8222

Some famous brands

Postal services

Most Post Offices are open Monday to Friday 9am to 5.30pm, and Saturday 9am to 12.30 or 1pm. For help and advice on all Post Office counter services, tel: 08457 22 33 44; www.postoffice.co.uk.

Lost and found

In the first instance, contact should be made with Strathclyde Police at Pitt Street *(see above)*.
Travel-related losses: for Central Station and Queen Street, tel: 0141 335 3276.
Buchanan Bus Station, tel: 0141 333 3708.

Museums and art galleries

Burrell Collection

Glasgow Museums controls a wonderful collection of municipal museums and galleries, many of which are mentioned in the *Places* section of this book. In general, they are open Monday to Thursday and Saturday 10am–5pm, Friday and Sunday 11am–5pm, and admission is free except in the cases of prestigious visiting exhibitions. For further information, tel: 0141 287 2699.

City guides

In the city centre, guides walk the main tourist areas with a brief to assist visitors. They have distinctive red-and-black uniforms with peaked caps, so don't be afraid to stop him or her and ask for help.

Cruising

The world's last surviving paddle steamer, the PS *Waverley*, has a home berth now at Pacific Quay (Glasgow Science Centre), tel: 0845 130 4647. A relic of the great days of steam, its massive engines are still open for inspection on summer cruises down the Firth of Clyde to Rothesay, Arran and the Kyles of Bute, www.waverleyexcursions.co.uk.

Sunday morning at St Alphonsus

Religion

All major religions are catered for, and the city has many beautiful and architecturally inspiring churches.

The Church of Scotland, which has responsibility for the magnificent Glasgow Cathedral, is contactable at the Presbytery of Glasgow, 260 Bath Street, tel: 0141 332 6606. **Roman Catholic**: The Archdiocese has modern offices beside the impressive St Andrew's Cathedral at 196 Clyde Street, tel: 0141 226 5898; **United Free Church of Scotland**, 11 Newton Place, tel: 0141 332 3435; **Islamic Centre**, Central Mosque, Mosque Avenue, tel: 0141 429 3132; **Buddhist Centre**, 329 Sauchiehall Street, tel: 0141 333 0524; **Hindu Temple**, 10 Great George Street, tel: 0141 332 0482; **Garnethill Synagogue**, 129 Hill Street, tel: 0141 332 4151.

Glasgow for Children

Glasgow is a city with attractions for all age ranges. The **Museum of Transport** at Kelvin Hall, 1 Bunhouse Road, tel: 0141 287 2720 (Monday to Thursday and Saturday 10am–5pm, Friday and Sunday 11am–5pm, *see page 40*), has a dazzling collection of vintage cars and motorbikes. Children can sit in a police van and in the cabin of an old steam train. There is also a full-scale street from the 1930s, with shops and a working cinema.

Trams at the Museum of Transport

Across the road, the newly refurbished **Kelvingrove Art Gallery and Museum**, tel: 0141 276 9599 (Monday to Thursday and Saturday 10am–5pm, Friday and Sunday 11am–5pm, *see page 39*), has a hands-on Environment Discovery Centre and a fabulous mini-museum for under-fives. From studying creepy-crawlies up close to staring into the jaws of a 13ft (4metre) high Ceratosaur, there's plenty to entertain the kids.

At the **Glasgow Science Centre**, (tel: 0141 420 5000, www.gsc.org.uk) there are four floors of hands-on exhibits in the Science Mall enable you to explore life's mysteries.

At **Hampden Park**, tel: 0141 616 6139; www.scottish footballmuseum.org.uk (Monday to Saturday 10am–5pm, Sunday 11am–5pm), Scotland's national football stadium, kids and adults alike will enjoy the Scottish Football Hall of Fame, and have an opportunity to tour the stadium.

Or you could enliven their school holidays by visiting **Scotland Street School Museum**, tel: 0141 287 0500 (Monday to Thursday and Saturday 10am–5pm, Friday and Sunday 11am–5pm, *see page 48*), an intriguing exhibition set in a Rennie Mackintosh building which will let them see how tough school used to be. The way Glasgow's adult daily life used to be is on display at **The Tenement House**, tel: 0844 493 2197 (March to October, daily 1pm–5pm, *see page 36*). Or, really going back in time, there is the **Fossil Grove** in Victoria Park, tel: 0141 950 1448 (Thursday to Monday 10am–5pm), where Glasgow's oldest attraction has fossilised trees dating back 330 million years.

Boys at Scotland Street School Museum

Out of town, 8 miles (13 km) away from Glasgow, **Mugdock Country Park**, tel: 0141 956 6100, has 500 acres (200 hectares) of moorland, woods, ruined castles and bike trails. **Kelburne Country Park**, near Largs (28 miles/45 km), tel: 01475 568 685, boasts waterfalls, falconry displays, an assault course and The Secret Forest. The refurbished **Summerlee Heritage Trust** at Coatbridge (9 miles/16km), tel: 01236 638460, offers kids the chance to ride on an old tram as part of Scotland's only electric-driven tramway. While out this way, the **Time Capsule** (14 miles/23km), tel: 01236 449572, with swimming and ice-skating among volcanoes and cavemen, is worth a visit.

Highland cattle

Accommodation

The Millennium

Hotels are plentiful in Glasgow and range from the exotic and astronomically priced to homely and sensible bed and breakfasts. Glasgow Tourist Information Centre, 11 George Square, tel: 0141 204 4400, provides an accommodation service. For a comprehensive list of hotels in the city, visit www.glasgowguide.co.uk/hotels.

Prices of hotels listed below vary seasonally, and the £-sign classifications are for two people in a double room on a bed-and-breakfast basis:

££££, over £130 per night; **£££**, over £90 per night; **££**, over £60 per night; **£**, under £60 per night.

££££

Crowne Plaza Glasgow, Congress Road, tel: 0141 306 9988. Major hotel on the riverside beside the SECC.

Glasgow Hilton, 1 William Street, tel: 0141 204 5555; www.hilton.co.uk/glasgow. Five-star hotel with over 300 rooms and all leisure and business facilities. Good restaurants.

Glasgow Marriot, 500 Argyle Street, tel: 0141 226 5577; www.marriot.com. International-style hotel at west end of city centre with all leisure and business facilities. Ten minutes' walk to Buchanan Street shops.

Hilton Glasgow Grosvenor, Great Western Road, tel: 0141 339 8811; www.hilton.co.uk/glasgowgrosvenor. Beautiful Venetian-inspired terrace opposite Botanic Gardens. Perfect for West End cafés and sights.

Hotel du Vin at One Devonshire Gardens, 1 Devonshire Gardens, Great Western Road, tel: 0141 339 2001; www.onedevonshiregardens.com. Superlative accommodation in an elegant tree-lined terrace. Professional service.

Mar Hall and Aveda Spa, Earl of Mar Estate, Renfrew, tel: 0141 812 9999; www.marhall.com. Stunning Gothic mansion just 10 minutes west of Glasgow airport.

The Millennium, 50 George Square, tel: 0141 332 6711; www.millenniumhotels.co.uk. Former railway hotel beside Queen Street fronting onto George Square.

Radisson SAS Hotel, Glasgow, 301 Argyle Street, tel: 0141 204 3333; www.radissonsas.com. This smart 250-room glass-fronted hotel is just a few footsteps from Glasgow Central Station and the main shopping district.

£££

ABode Glasgow, 129 Bath Street, tel: 0141 221 6789; www.abodehotels.co.uk. This central boutique hotel combines stunning modern and traditional (Edwardian) architecture with comfort and a top-class restaurant. Stylish.

City Inn, Finnieston Quay, tel: 0141 240 1002; www.cityinn.com/glasgow. A stylish yet comfortable place to stay, with a fresh contemporary design and right at the riverside.

Crowne Plaza Glasgow

Hotel du Vin at One Devonshire Gardens

Corus Hotel, Glasgow, 377 Argyle Street, tel: 0141 245 2700; www.corushotels.co.uk. A central, modern hotel.
Langs Hotel, 2 Port Dundas Place, tel: 0141 333 5712; www.langshotels.co.uk. A chilled modern vibe and a central location make this another mid-priced winner.
Malmaison, 278 West George Street, tel: 0141 572 1000; www.malmaison.com. Rooms with individual character in an attractive clubby atmosphere. Stunning architecture.

££

Ambassador Hotel, 7 Kelvin Drive, tel: 0141 946 1018. Quality bed and breakfast in private hotel near the Botanic Gardens and handy for the West End.
Argyll Hotel, 973 Sauchiehall Street, tel: 0141 337 3313; www.argyllhotelglasgow.co.uk. Period hotel across from Kelvingrove Park with good Scottish food in Sutherlands Restaurant. A home from home.
Best Western, 27 Elmbank Street, tel: 0141 227 2772. Old town-house building in excellent location.
Cathedral House, 28–32 Cathedral Square, tel: 0141 552 3519; www.cathedralhouse.com. Unusual hotel in Victorian setting near historical attractions of old Glasgow.
Kirklee Hotel, 11 Kensington Gate, tel: 0141 334 5555; www.kirkleehotel.co.uk. Attractive hotel in Edwardian terrace with pleasant gardens. Ideally situated for West End.
Quality Central Hotel, Gordon Street, tel: 0141 221 9680. Victorian ex-railway hotel beside Central Station in splendid position for city-centre shops.

£

Albion Hotel, 405–407 North Woodside Road, tel: 0141 339 8620. Pleasant, small hotel in West End area. Good for sights and cafés.
Express by Holiday Inn, 122 Stockwell Street, tel: 0141 548 5000. 128-bedroom hotel close to the River Clyde and St Enoch Shopping Centre. Budget comfort.
Glasgow Youth Hostel, 8 Park Terrace, tel: 0870 004 1119; www.syha.org.uk. Excellent location. You won't find better value to be in touching distance of key sites.
The Heritage Hotel, 4–5 Alfred Terrace, tel: 0141 339 6955. Close to all West End attractions, offering comfort in a grand Victorian setting.
Kelvin Hotel, 15 Buckingham Terrace, tel: 0141 339 7143; www.kelvinhotel.com. Family-owned hotel in the West End within impressive Victorian building.
The Piping Centre, 30–34 McPhater Street, tel: 0141 353 5551; www.thepipingcentre.co.uk. Only eight rooms in this comfortable hotel commanding the top end of Hope Street.
Rennie Mackintosh Hotel, 218–220 Renfrew Street, tel: 0141 333 9992. Tribute hotel to Glasgow's favourite architect and decorated in his unique style.

Cathedral House detail

79

The Rennie Mackintosh

Index
